books designed with giving in mind

Vegetable Cookbook	First Brandy Cookbook	Paris...and then some
Kid's Arts and Crafts	Cheese Guide & Cookbook	Sunday Breakfast
Bread Baking	Miller's German	Fisherman's Wharf Cookbook
The Crockery Pot Cookbook	Quiche & Souffle	Ice Cream Cookbook
Kid's Garden Book	To My Daughter, With Love	Hippo Hamburger
Classic Greek Cooking	Natural Foods	Blender Cookbook
The Compleat American	Chinese Vegetarian	The Wok, a Chinese Cookbook
Housewife 1776	Four Seasons Party Book	Christmas Cookbook
Low Carbohydrate Cookbook	Jewish Gourmet	Cast Iron Cookbook
The World In One Meal	Working Couples	Japanese Country
Kid's Cookbook	Mexican	Fondue Cookbook
Italian		

from nitty gritty productions

DEDICATION

To the gracious, hospitable proprietors of four fascinating restaurants in Italy, a special "thank you" for expanding my horizons not only in Italian cuisine, but in international friendship and goodwill as well.

Ristorante "Peoceto Risorto"   - Venice

Ristorante Noemi   - Venice

Ristorante 13 Gobbi   - Florence

Ristorante Tana del Grillo   - Rome

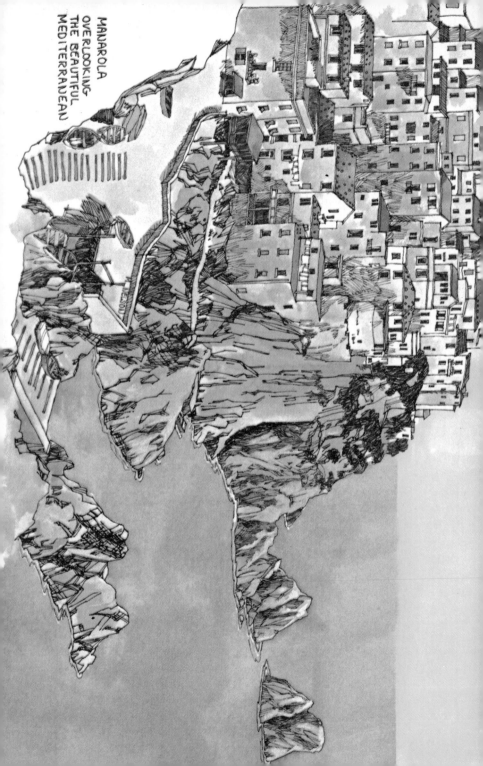

MANAROLA
OVERLOOKING
THE BEAUTIFUL
MEDITERRANEAN

the ITALIAN COOKBOOK

by KATHERINE RAMANO

Illustrated by MIKE NELSON

© Copyright 1973
Nitty Gritty Productions
Concord, California

A Nitty Gritty Book*
Published by
Nitty Gritty Productions
P. O. Box 5457
Concord, California 94524

*Nitty Gritty Books — Trademark
Owned by Nitty Gritty Productions
Concord, California

ISBN 0-911954-27-9

CONTENTS

THE FOUNTAIN OF TREVI
TRADITION PROMISES
THE VISITOR WHO
THROWS A COIN
INTO THESE WATERS
THAT HE WILL
RETURN TO ROME

FOREWORD

Listening to conversation of individuals who have traveled in Italy is much like listening to the story of the four blind men describing an elephant—each has his own impression and each is enchanted with a different facet. The ruins of antiquity, the medieval architecture, the art wonders that abound, the everchanging landscape ranging from wild mountain regions to gently rounded symmetrical hills to monotonous plains, all have inspired thousands of books to be written. One of the wonders of Italy is, of course, the food! And one cannot, in one book, begin to cover all of the gustatory delights which the Italian enjoys because, like the landscape, the cuisine changes drastically from region to region, from north to south, from mountain to seashore.

Against such grand backgrounds of art, nature, architecture, and history, the Italian goes about the business of living with a zest and lack of inhibition which astounds and delights the more reticent American. What else but a keen sense of drama could prompt the artistry shown by street vendors in arranging the goods on their barrows, whether it be fruit, vegetables, fish, lace, or jewelry. This same sense of drama produces the ferocious uproar of the Italian street—the shrill vocal encounters, ear-splitting blasts of horns, the screech and gear-grinding sounds of bus, car, and lorry—and can even be detected in the Italian's air of unutterable boredom in a piazza on a Sunday afternoon.

People walk more in Italy—in fact, in all of Europe—than we do in America. The traffic is always a hazard, but no one seems to pay much attention to it. People of all ages are seen promenading, window shopping, greeting people on the street and chatting. The hours for this activity are usually between six and eight p.m. Dinner begins at about 8:30, so the walk is good for the digestion, appetite, and general well-being.

Coffee bars are everywhere throughout Italy. The national drink is espresso, often served in special-size cups which are slightly larger than demitasse cups. These cafes serve cornetti or rolls in the morning and tiny very sweet pastries in the afternoon. It is said that Italians drink just enough espresso in the morning to make them nervous. The cafes almost always serve liquor or aperitifs as well as coffee. Watching people stroll by is a national pastime for most Europeans and Italians are no exception. Life is more relaxed and people take time out to read, chat, and observe life from the tables surrounding the cafes. They provide a welcome break for the tourist and native alike.

To an American, Italian food means Pizza, Chicken Cacciatore, Lasagna, and Spaghetti with loads of tomato sauce. It conjures up the gustatory delights of herbs, spices, garlic, onions, and olive oil. But that is not the real picture. Because of the importance in her history of the city-states, the cities as well as entire regions of Italy have their own specialties. Venice has magnificent seafood, with a delicacy of preparation and presentation to rival the famous architecture. Florence prepares steak which easily competes with the beef Scotland or Iowa has to offer. Rome has such a multiplicity of cuisine from all over Italy that the mind and stomach cannot comprehend it all.

You can buy freshly made cheeses, selecting them from where they hang on the facade of a latteria. So delicate are their flavors that you will not relate them

A FLOWER STAND ON THE
SPANISH STEPS
ROME

to Italian cheeses you have tasted in the United States. The Italian ham is so un-like the American variety that with your eyes closed you will find it difficult to recognize it as such.

Food in Italy is admired not only for its taste but also for its esthetic appeal.

It is displayed to delight the eye. Restaurants often have their fresh—often live—seafood or fish on display. Fruit and desserts are in prominent places of honor, with the desserts frequently on wheeled carts which are brought to the table when you wish to make a selection. These same carts also carry beautiful assortments of appetizers. In some areas, strings of sausages festoon the doorways from the foyer into the restaurant. During the course of the serving hours, the sausages are taken down and cooked as they are ordered. A trattoria will often display the various cuts of meat and vegetables in a glass case in the entry. This is a combination of storage and a way of letting you see what is on the menu. Restaurants like Noemi in Venice have magnificent arrangements of seafoods in their front window. A small trattoria in Rome features a trestle table the length of

the room laden with salads, fresh fruits, fresh fish, and other delicacies to tempt the eye and palate. Fresh flowers decorate the tables in even the smallest establishment. Tablecloths and cloth napkins have not yet been replaced by formica and paper. There is a special mood.

The trattoria differs from a ristorante in that a trattoria has no pretentions, preserves a more home-like atmosphere and is, in fact, often run by a family. Prices in a trattoria are more moderate, generally, than in a ristorante. Some trattorie are quite simple while others have more modern accoutrements.

The Italian meal is lengthy and is to be relaxed into—to be savored. There is never any rush. Not only will you never be rushed from your table but the relaxed atmosphere is so pervasive, you may find it difficult to get your check when you are ready to leave. This is often interpreted by Americans as poor service. The Italian way of eating and relaxing takes some "getting into" for the American geared to a quick lunch and on to the next appointment.

Everyone eats two large meals daily. Breakfast, at most, is a cup of espresso or cappuccino and a hard roll. (Cappuccino is espresso combined with steamed milk.) The large meals are a relaxing experience with foods served course by course. Ample time is allowed between courses to relax. Since businesses are closed from 12:30 to 3:30, families gather for both large meals.

The typical meal begins with an antipasto followed by either soup or a pasta; then the main dish accompanied by a vegetable or perhaps a salad; following the main dish, a dessert of fruit and cheese and, finally, espresso. At this point, liqueurs may also be served. The typical meal takes about 1 1/2 to 2 hours to consume in even the simplest restaurant.

I hope you will enjoy the recipes in this book and expand your own ideas of Italian cooking. The foods included here are perhaps not what you imagine to be Italian—but try them! They will bring you some of the diversity of the delectable cuisine of Italy.

MEDIEVAL
STONE BRIDGE
SPANS THE NEVA
RIVER BESIDE
ZUCCARELLO

Appetizers

Best known of the appetizers is Parma ham, also called prosciutto, which is usually served with a wedge of ripe melon for a delightful contrast in taste. Fresh figs, grown in this part of the world for thousands of years, are combined with paper thin slices of salami, or a slice of Prague ham is eaten with a slice of fresh bread.

In port cities, seafood is the preferred appetizer and, although seafood of the Mediterranean or Adriatic differs from our American varieties, you can still prepare the recipe for Antipasto alla Noemi, for example, and find it tastes very much like the delicately flavored original.

No appetizer list is complete without mention of the beautiful Antipasto Misto al Carrello. This mosaic of colors and flavors is served on a cart wheeled to the table, a great idea for entertaining. So begin your Italian meal as the Italians do with one of the following recipes.

HOT DIPPING SAUCE (WITH VEGETABLES)
BAGNA CAUDA

The contrast between hot sauce and cold crisp vegetables provides the taste-buds of the diner with provocative stimulation for the meal ahead.

Select vegetables from Group A and Group B. Vegetables in Group A are cut into 1/2" x 3" strips. Those in Group B are served whole. Clean them, crisp them in ice water for 1 1/2 hours, then drain on paper towels. Arrange attractively on a platter or in bowls, cover with plastic wrap and refrigerate until serving time.

GROUP A   GROUP B

peeled, seeded cucumbers   scallions (green onions)
green peppers   small mushrooms
peeled carrots   cauliflowerets
zucchini   broccoli flowerets

Sauce

2-2oz. cans of flat anchovies
3/4 cup olive oil
pinch dry hot mustard
8 peeled cloves garlic
2 tbs. white wine vinegar

Place all ingredients in the blender. Puree, then simmer for about 30 minutes before serving. Serve in an earthenware casserole which can be kept warm on an electric hottray or over a Sterno heater. The icy vegetables are dunked in this hot sauce before eating. Bread sticks may be served as an accompaniment. Supply plenty of napkins for your guests when serving this appetizer/sauce combination.

ITALIAN HAM AND MELON
PROSCIUTTO E MELONE

Using peeled wedges of fully-ripened cantaloupe, Casaba, honeydew, or Persian melon, serve one 2" wedge per person. Drape 2 paper-thin slices of prosciutto (Parma ham) over each melon wedge. There are about 4 to 5 slices of prosciutto per quarter pound. The flavor of the melon is best when served at room temperature. Have a peppermill readily available so guests may season this dish to their own tastes.

If you can locate Prague ham to use in place of the prosciutto, do so. It is highly prized by many Italian gourmets for its delicate flavor. It can be served alone or with the melon as described above.

STUFFED ZUCCHINI SLICES
RIPIENI ZUCCHINI ALLA 13 GOBBI

7-8 zucchini about 2" in diameter
1/3 cup bread crumbs
1/3 cup grated imported Swiss cheese

1/2 cup ground cooked chicken
olive oil
salt, pepper, and Italian herb blend

Thoroughly wash the zucchini. Place in a large pot containing enough salted water to cover and simmer for 6 to 8 minutes or until they are slightly firm but not quite tender. Trim away the ends of each zucchini and cut the remaining part into 1" slices. Using a small spoon, carefully scoop out the center of each slice, leaving a 1/4" base to hold the stuffing. As commercial crumbs are too fine, make bread crumbs in the blender from stale French bread.

Combine the crumbs, cheese, and chicken with just enough oil to barely bind the mixture together. Season well with salt, pepper, and a good Italian herb blend. Carefully spoon about 2 teaspoons of stuffing into, and mounded on, each zucchini slice. Place the Ripieni on a greased baking sheet and bake in a preheated 350° oven just until piping hot. Serve hot or at toom temperature. Makes 36 slices.

13

SALAD OF THE TYROL
INSALATA ALLA TYROLESE

This dish originated in the Italian Tyrol and is very popular throughout northern Italy. The Tyrol is that portion of the north that borders on both Switzerland and Austria.

4 Bratwurst Sausages
Beer
3/4 lb. finely minced ham
1/2 cup cooked broccoli flowerets
1/2 cup cooked, finely minced carrots
1/2 cup cooked, minced cauliflowerets
1/2 cup finely minced celery
1/2 cup finely minced fennel
1/2 cup cooked petit pois (tiny peas)
2 tbs. drained capers
Homemade Mayonnaise (p. 15)
Dijon mustard to taste

Fry the bratwurst over low-to-medium heat until lighly browned on all sides, turning frequently. Remove the bratwurst from the skillet, place in a saucepan and add enough beer to almost cover the sausages. Cover and simmer for 20 minutes. Remove bratwurst from the beer, cool and cut into thin slices. Add enough

mustard to the mayonnaise to give a hint of mustard flavor without overpowering it. Combine all ingredients (including bratwurst slices) adding just enough mayonnaise to bind all the ingredients together. Serve at room temperature, adding the mayonnaise just before serving. Serves 8.

HOMEMADE MAYONNAISE
SALSA MAIONESE

1 large egg
1 tsp. Dijon mustard

3 tbs. lemon juice
1 cup olive oil

1 tsp. salt

Put everything but the oil in the blender jar. Add 1/3 cup oil, cover, and blend at high speed for about 5 seconds. Remove the center part of the cover and add the remaining oil in a slow, steady drizzle. Continue to blend until thick and smooth. Makes over 1 cup.

MIXED APPETIZERS SERVED FROM A CART
ANTIPASTO MISTO AL CARRETTO

The colorful antipasto (before the food) is the Italian's hors d'oeuvre. This selection is served on a cart with each food in its own dish.

4 large ripe sliced tomatoes
1 can tiny sardines
1 cup cooked squid (p. 18)
1 cup sour imported gherkins
1/2 cup tiny pickled onions
1 cup tiny cooked shrimp

1/2 cup thin strips sweet red pepper
1 can anchovy fillets
1 cup black and green olives
1/4 recipe Insalate alla Tirolese (p.14,15) (using potato and green beans instead of cauliflower and broccoli)
1 can imported mushrooms packed in oil

Serve each food item separately—in a bowl or on a plate, whichever is suitable for the particular food. Arrange the serving dishes with color contrasts in mind. Each person makes his own selection. Suggested accompaniments: French bread, butter, and wine. Serves 8.

LIVER PATE ON BREAD ROUNDS
CROSTINI ALLA PISANA

This is a delicious, slightly grainy paté. The bread rounds may be toasted or, if you prefer, spread it on crackers.

1/2 lb. chicken livers
3 tbs. butter
brandy to taste

heavy cream
French or Italian bread about
    2" in diameter, sliced 1/2" thick

Trim the livers, removing fat and membranes. Wash and pat thoroughly dry on paper towels. Heat the butter in a skillet over medium heat and sauté the livers, turning on all sides, until they lose their redness. Lower the heat, add a little brandy to taste, cover and simmer for 10 minutes or until completely cooked. Cool. Put the livers through a food grinder using a fine blade. Add just enough cream to loosely bind the mixture. Spread each bread slice with the liver paté. It will seem slightly dry. Serve at room temperature. Delicious!

APPETIZERS, NOEMI STYLE
ANTIPASTO ALLA NOEMI

Venetian cooking allows the delicate flavor of the seafood full rein. This antipasto is actually a filling first course.

1 lb. squid (optional)
white wine
24 fresh mussels in the shell or fresh oysters in the shell
16 cooked crab claws
1 lb. freshly cooked lobster meat
16 cooked, peeled, large shrimp
1 lb. cooked, peeled, medium shrimp
1/2 lb. cooked tiny shrimp
16 lemon wedges
3/4 cup olive oil
1/4 cup fresh lemon juice
1 can imported mushrooms packed in oil

1 recipe Homemade Mayonnaise (p. 15)
1/3 cup catsup

brandy to taste
Worcestershire sauce to taste

Have your fish dealer prepare the squid (skin, remove the long bone on the inside, the yellow deposit, and the ink sac). Wash the squid well, dry thoroughly, and cut crosswise into 1/4″ slices resembling rings. Poach in white wine to cover just until tender. Drain. Cool to room temperature.

Thoroughly wash and scrub the mussels, removing grit and sand. Place the mussels in a large pot. Pour in 1/2 cup boiling water, cover, and steam over medium heat for 5 minutes or until the shells open. They should be cooked and served the same day you buy them.

Arrange an assortment of the seafood attractively on 8 plates. Garnish with lemon wedges. Whisk together the oil and lemon juice, and drizzle the mixture over the seafood. Using a whisk, combine the mayonnaise, catsup, brandy, and Worcestershire sauce. Serve a dollop of this sauce on each plate. Makes 8 servings.

A TIGHT SQUEEZE
VENICE

Soups

Minestra—or Minestrone—is the most famous of the Italian soups. The story is told that centuries ago, when no trattorie or ristoranti existed in Italy, the brothers in the monasteries offered hospitality to travelers. So there would always be food ready for any such "drop-in" guests, they kept a special guest-kettle on the fire. Into this kettle went meat, vegetables, pasta, beans, and seasonings, thus originating this zestful and nourishing soup.

Even today, soup plays an important role in Italian main meals. It must be full-flavored and well-seasoned and soups such as Minestra con Würstel and Zuppa di Verdura con Croutons are thick with assorted vegetables.

Basic soup stocks are well worth the time and effort required to make them as they may also be used in gravies or sauces and add flavor to casseroles and meat dishes. The versatility and adaptability of soup is limited only by the creativity of the cook and the variety of vegetables, meats, and seasonings available. Soup's on!

CHICKEN BROTH
BRODO DI POLLO

6 lb. assortment of chicken backs, necks, and wings
2 1/2 qts. water or just enough to cover the chicken
2 stalks celery with leaves
1 bunch of washed Italian parsley (flat leaves)

3 peeled onions
1 clove garlic
salt to taste
2 peeled, trimmed carrots

Rinse the chicken in several changes of cold water. Remove excess fat. Place the chicken and the water in a 12-quart pot, bring to a boil, lower the heat, and simmer. After 5 minutes, remove the scum from the surface. Continue to cook for 2 to 3 hours. Add the remaining ingredients and simmer for another hour. Remove from heat, correct seasoning, and pour the broth through a strainer into a 6-quart pot. Cool, cover, and refrigerate overnight. The next day remove the congealed fat from the surface of the broth. Reheat and pour the broth through a strainer lined with several layers of clean cheesecloth. This further clarifies the liquid. Now it can be frozen or it may be refrigerated for up to 3 days. Makes 2 to 2 1/2 quarts of chicken stock.

BEEF BROTH
BRODO DI MANZO

6 lbs. beef bones, including some marrow bones
4-5 lbs. very lean short ribs
2 peeled, trimmed carrots
2 stalks celery with leaves
1 bunch of washed Italian parsley (flat leaves)

2 1/2 qts. water
3 peeled onions
1 clove garlic
salt to taste

Thoroughly rinse the bones and meat and drain well on paper towels. Place the bones and ribs in a single layer in a large shallow roasting pan. Bake in a preheated 425° oven until the bones and meat are browned. This gives the stock a rich color. Then place the bones and meat in a 12-quart pot, bring to a boil, lower the heat, and simmer. Remove any scum that forms on the surface of the broth. Continue to cook for 2 to 3 hours. Add the remaining ingredients and simmer for another hour. Remove from heat, correct seasoning to taste, and pour the broth through a strainer into a 6-quart pot. Cool, cover, and refrigerate overnight. The following day remove the congealed fat from the surface of the broth. Reheat and

23

pour the broth through a strainer lined with several layers of clean cheesecloth to further clarify the liquid. Now it can be frozen or it may be refrigerated for up to 3 days. This recipe makes about 2 1/2 quarts of beef stock.

SOUP WITH SAUSAGE
MINESTRA CON SALCICCIA

We enjoyed this hearty one-dish meal—along with a good Italian red wine and crusty fresh bread—at a small trattoria in the shadow of the Tyrol. I'm sure you will find it just as enjoyable and delicious in your own home.

9 thick, chopped slices of bacon
3 large onions, finely chopped
1/2 cup pearl rice
4 stalks celery, finely chopped

4 carrots, peeled, chopped
6 potatoes, finely chopped
1 lb. can tomato puree
2 1/2 qts. water
8 to 10 links of Polish sausage

Saute the bacon in a 12-quart pot over medium heat. When some fat has been rendered, add the onions, sautéeing until tender. Add rice, toss until coated with fat, then add the remaining ingredients, except the sausage. Gradually bring to a boil, stirring occasionally. Lower the heat, cover, and simmer for 1 1/2 hours. Stir from time to time. About 40 minutes before serving, add 1 sausage per person. In Italy you cut the sausage in the soup plate, then proceed to eat it with a soup spoon. Makes 8 to 10 generous servings. This is even tastier if prepared the previous day. In that case do not add the sausage until you have reheated the soup. Served with red wine and French bread, this provides a hearty meal.

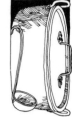

SOUP WITH GREENS AND CROUTONS
ZUPPA DI VERDURA CON CROUTONS

A delightfully zesty vegetable soup.

1/2 cup dried fava beans or 3 large potatoes
4 carrots
3 large onions
6 zucchini
3 stalks celery
1/2 of a small head of cabbage
2 1/2 qts. of water
salt
freshly ground pepper to taste
1 bay leaf
10 to 12 half-inch thick slices of toasted French bread
freshly grated Parmesan cheese

Soak the fava beans in a generous amount of water for 24 hours. Drain and remove the skins. (If fava beans are not available, substitute peeled, cubed potatoes.)

Peel and cube the carrots and onions. Trim and cube the celery. Trim and cut the zucchini into half-inch slices. Core and finely shred the cabbage. Place the vegetables and water in a 12-quart pot. Add more water if needed to cover the vegetables. Season to taste, add the bay leaf and bring to a boil. Cover, lower the heat, and simmer for 1 1/2 to 2 hours. Remove the bay leaf and correct the seasoning to taste. Cool and refrigerate overnight. Reheat prior to serving. Place a piece of toasted French bread in each soup bowl. Carefully ladle the soup over the "crouton." Serve grated Parmesan cheese for diners to add according to their taste. Makes 10 to 12 generous servings.

PEASANT SOUP
ZUPPA ALLA PAESANS NEL TEGAME

This delicious extra thick variation of Zuppa di Verdura was served to us in a trattoria in Florence.

Prepare Zuppa di Verdura (p.26) omitting the toasted bread and Parmesan cheese. Serve with almost no broth. This is easily done by using a slotted spoon to serve the soup. Serves 6 to 8. Freeze the unused broth for future use.

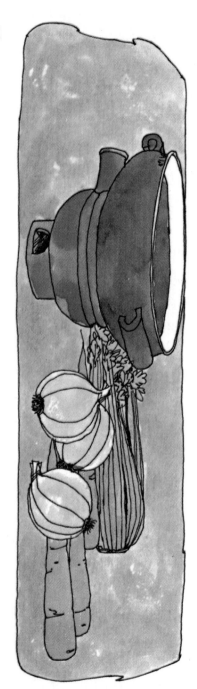

CHICKEN SOUP, PAVIA STYLE
ZUPPA PAVESE

Although eggs are often used in soups, this recipe calls for a whole egg to be placed atop a slice of toasted French bread in each bowl—an unusual and tasty soup variation.

8 slices French bread cut 1 1/2" thick
1/3 cup melted sweet butter
2 qts. beef broth (p.23)

8 large very fresh eggs, poached
   freshly grated Parmesan cheese
   salt to taste

Toast the bread in the oven. Brush with the melted butter and place a slice in each warmed soup bowl. Bring the broth almost to a boil. Carefully break 1 egg into a cup and slide it onto a bread slice. Repeat with the remaining eggs. Sprinkle each egg with grated cheese and lightly salt each egg. Quickly and carefully ladle 1 cup of boiling broth into each bowl over the egg. The stock poaches the egg. Makes 8 servings.

FISH CONSOMME, AVE MARIA
ZUPPA DI PESCE, AVE MARIA

This rosy Venetian soup has a very delicate flavor.

Bones, heads and trimmings of
  6 to 8 white-fleshed fish
2 qts. water
2 large trimmed celery stalks
1 large thickly-sliced onion

3 sprigs parsley
2 large ripe tomatoes, peeled, seeded, and diced
salt to taste
1/4 cup tiny pasta (anellini, stelline or ditali)

Place all ingredients except the salt and pasta in a 6-quart pot. Bring to a boil, cover, lower the heat, and simmer for 1 hour. Skim if necessary. Cool slightly and pour through a fine strainer lined with several thicknesses of clean cheesecloth. Season VERY DELICATELY. Do not overpower the flavor of the fish. Cook the pasta in 2 quarts boiling salted water. When it is barely tender, pour 2 cups cold water into the pot and drain through a fine strainer. Divide the pasta among 6 soup bowls and pour the soup over the pasta. Makes 6 attractive servings.

FISH SOUP
ZUPPA DI PESCE

Accompanied by white wine and fresh Italian bread, this seafood soup is a complete meal.

Zuppa Ave Maria (p. 30) omitting the pasta
1 crushed garlic clove
2 sprigs finely minced parsley
tabasco sauce to taste
1 lb. crab, cut into pieces
1/2 lb. squid prepared for cooking

6 mussels, well-scrubbed
1 lb. of lobster, cut into pieces
6 clams, well-scrubbed
1/2 lb. red snapper cut into 1 1/2" pieces
1/2 lb. halibut cut into 1 1/2" pieces
1/2 lb. sea bass cut into 1 1/2" pieces

Add the garlic, parsley, and tabasco sauce to the fish broth. This gives the broth a piquant flavor for this dish. Add the seafood and simmer, half covered, over the lowest possible heat for 2 hours. Serve in large shallow soup bowls. Serves 6.

ITALIAN TYROL
BEAUTIFUL MOUNTAINS
IN NORTHERN ITALY

Salads & Vegetables

Fresh vegetables are prepared quite simply for the Italian table. They are cooked just to the point of being easy to chew but not soggy—al dente—as with pastas. Asparagus is often served as a separate course. The eggplant recipes may be prepared either as separate vegetable courses or as appetizers. The other vegetable dishes are usually served as side dishes accompanying the main course. The appropriate vegetable is selected for its taste, texture, and color contrast in combination with the rest of the meal.

A wide variety of greens—dandelion leaves, many varieties of lettuce, fennel and others often overlooked by the American cook—are used by the Italians for their salads, which are rarely dressed before being served. Cruets of olive oil and wine vinegar are on the table for each person to use as they please. Salads are simple and made with the freshest vegetables available.

The many greens which may be strange to your taste in your salad may also

turn up cooked as a vegetable or as part of a vegetable dish. They are worth trying—not just for their novelty but for their tart flavor which complements entrees of broiled meat or chicken. Unusual vegetables such as scorzonera root or wild asparagus are to be found on Italian tables, but not with the frequency of spinach, peas, beans, asparagus, or tomatoes. Beets, Swiss chard, carrots, broccoli, and brussels sprouts also find a place on the Italian menu. Chestnuts are found in abundance, used in vegetable dishes, stuffings, or pureed. Vendors also sell them hot and roasted.

Mushrooms, tomatoes, peppers, eggplants, and squash are the mainstays in Roman vegetable dishes. Their flavors blend and mingle with the meats, cheeses, herbs and breads. There are a great variety of mushrooms available to the Italian cook, some large enough for stuffing. These flavorful fungi, with their ruffles and spots, are sometimes placed in baskets inside the trattorie to add their colors of cream, buff, orange, and brown to the already enticing arrays of food.

FAVA (BROAD) BEANS
FAVE

These Italian favorites resemble lima beans but are somewhat larger. If you can buy dried fava beans, soak them for 24 hours in water to cover. Remove all the skins—they slip off very easily. Cook in salted water or in bouillon for about 45 to 50 minutes, until tender. Serve with sweet butter.

BEANS IN CREAM
FAVE IN CREMA

4 cups fava beans, cooked and well-drained   1/4 cup sweet butter
salt and freshly ground pepper to taste   2 cups heavy cream

Heat the butter, add the beans and gently toss them, coating them in butter on all sides. Add the heavy cream and cook over medium heat for 15 to 20 minutes. The cream will thicken. Season to taste with salt and pepper and serve hot. Serves 5 to 6.

BEANS, ROMAN STYLE
FAVE ALLA ROMANA

If you cannot find dried fava beans in your area, shop a specialty grocery store for canned, cooked fava beans. If they are unavailable in either form, dried lima beans may be substituted.

4 cups fava beans cooked and well-drained (p.34)

2 tbs. butter

4 large ripe tomatoes peeled, seeded and diced

salt

freshly ground pepper to taste

Sauté the tomato strips in hot butter over medium heat for 10 minutes. Lightly season to taste. Place a large spoonful of tomatoes on each serving of beans. Pass the remaining sauce for those who prefer an additional amount. Serves 5 to 6.

MIXED SALAD
INSALATA CAPRICCIOSA

This basic salad is included on most restaurant menus throughout Italy.

torn lettuce
tomato slices
julienne-cut cold cooked vegetables such as carrots or zucchini
olive oil
vinegar

Arrange the ingredients attractively on a bed of lettuce placed on a plate or in a shallow bowl. Serve the oil and vinegar in cruets at the table so each diner may add dressing in any amount according to taste.

TOMATO SALAD
INSALATA DI POMODORO

Large, ruby-red slices of beefsteak tomatoes are the star attraction, with the added features in the seasonings.

1 large ripe sliced tomato for each serving
salt
freshly ground pepper
crushed fresh basil to taste
Olive oil and red wine vinegar in separate cruets

The tomatoes should be at room temperature. Slice and serve them attractively arranged on individual salad plates. Lightly season to taste. Each person adds oil and vinegar just before eating the salad.

CHICORY SALAD
INSALATA CHICORIA FALCONE

This is a marvelous salad to accompany a filling main course.

2 lbs. fresh chicory
2 tbs. olive oil
oil
salt
freshly ground pepper to taste
4 lemon wedges

For the best flavor, chicory should be prepared and used within a day of its purchase. Wash the chicory, drain it well, and chop finely. Sauté the chicory in hot oil over medium heat for about 3 minutes, just until limp. Serve at room temperature on salad plates. Season to taste with salt and pepper. Lightly drizzle each serving with olive oil. Accompany with a lemon wedge. Serves 4.

BROCCOLI, CALABRIA STYLE
BROCCOLI CALABRESE

This is an unusual Italian treatment of a popular American vegetable.

1 1/2 lbs. fresh broccoli
2 tbs. olive oil
2 crushed cloves garlic
salt, freshly ground pepper to taste

3 large ripe tomatoes, peeled,
    seeded, and diced
2 tbs. plumped raisins
1/4 cup pine nuts

Trim and rinse the broccoli, then poach it in 6 quarts boiling salted water for 10 to 15 minutes—until tender but still crunchy. While the broccoli is cooking, sauté the garlic in oil over medium heat. Add tomatoes, plus the salt and pepper to taste, and simmer for 15 to 20 minutes.

Drain the broccoli, remove the flowerets and place them on a warm platter. Finely dice the stalks and place them with the flowerets on the platter. Now add the raisins and nuts to the tomato mixture and cook an additional 2 to 3 minutes. Pour this sauce over the broccoli. Serves 6 to 8.

HARBOR OF PORTOFINO
SHELTERING SEAFARERS
SINCE ROMAN TIMES

SPINACH IN BUTTER
SPINACI IN BURRO

This simple method of preparing spinach preserves all the flavor of the vegetable.

2 lbs. fresh young spinach
salt, pepper, and nutmeg to taste
1/4 cup sweet butter at room temperature

Wash the spinach in several changes of cold water. DO NOT USE AN ALUMINUM POT as it produces a bitter taste. Instead, place the clean spinach in a heavy-bottomed enamel pot with 1 tablespoon sweet butter and a tiny bit of salt. Cover and cook over high heat, turning it over from time to time. It is done when all the spinach is wilted. Drain, place in an old linen towel and squeeze out all the excess moisture. Chop the spinach, and place it in a heavy skillet over low heat with all the remaining butter. When the butter melts, gently toss the spinach to thoroughly butter it. Season very lightly. Serves 6.

PEAS AND ITALIAN HAM
PISELLINI AL PROSCIUTTO

This attractive dish is included on almost every restaurant menu in Italy.

1/4 cup sweet butter
1 small onion finely minced
1/4 lb. prosciutto or smoked ham
1 10-oz. pkg. frozen petit pois (tiny peas)

Melt the sweet butter in a heavy skillet over medium heat. Sauté the onion and ham until the onion is soft but not browned, add the frozen peas, and tightly cover the pan. Check occasionally to see if they are tender. It should take 5 to 10 minutes. Using this method, the vegetable stays beautifully green and retains all its flavor. Serves 5 to 6.

ASPARAGUS ITALIAN STYLE
ASPARAGI ALL' ITALIANA

Asparagus is presented here as a separate course.

2 1/2 lbs. fresh asparagus

1/2 cup freshly grated Parmesan cheese

1/4 lb. sweet butter

Almost the entire asparagus spear can be used when it is prepared this way. Trim the ends. Using a sharp paring knife, peel each spear so that the tender part is exposed. When you are done, the spear should be pale green with the same thickness from stem to tip. Tie the spears in bundles of 6 or 7 each and lay the bundles flat in an oblong pot. Cover with salted water and bring to a boil. Lower the heat and simmer about 12 minutes for young spears and 16 to 18 minutes for thick spears. Asparagus should be just tender but never limp. When a knife easily penetrates the stems, the asparagus is done. Drain and blot on a linen towel, place the bundles on a hot platter and remove the strings. Sprinkle with cheese and dot with butter. Serves 6.

ASPARAGUS WITH MAYONNAISE
ASPARAGI CON MAIONESE

Cook and drain as directed. Cool to room temperature. Serve with Home-made Mayonnaise (p.15).

ASPARAGUS APPIA STYLE
ASPARAGI APPIA

Cook and drain as directed and place the asparagus on a hot platter. Sprinkle with 2 finely chopped hard-cooked eggs. Season with salt and pepper and drizzle with 1/3 cup melted sweet butter.

ASPARAGUS MILAN STYLE
ASPARAGI MILANESE

Cook and drain as directed and arrange the asparagus on a hot platter. Sprinkle with 2 tablespoons finely minced parsley. Lightly drizzle olive oil over the asparagus, season with salt and pepper, and serve with lemon wedges.

DEEP FRIED EGGPLANT
MELANZANE FRITTI

If you like eggplant, you will love this recipe. Prepared this way, it can serve as either an appetizer or an entree.

6 large eggs
1/2 tsp. salt
tabasco sauce to taste
1 1/3 cups light cream or half and half

1/2 cup flour
2 peeled eggplants
salt

Beat the eggs, salt, tabasco sauce, and cream together until well mixed. Add the flour and beat with a whisk until smooth. Cover and refrigerate for 2 hours. Cut the eggplant into 1/2" thick slices. Generously salt both sides of each eggplant slice, placing them on several thicknesses of paper towels. Put a pastry board on top of the eggplant slices and weight it with 4 to 5 large cans of juice or fruit for 1 hour, then rinse slices thoroughly under cold running water. Drain on more paper towels and pat dry.

Remove batter from refrigerator and beat well before using. Preheat a deep fryer filled with 3 pounds of shortening to 375°. Dip the eggplant slices, one at a time, into the batter to coat. Fry in the fat until they are browned and crisp. Drain on paper towels and serve immediately. Serves 6.

ARTICHOKES FLORENTINE
CARCIOFI FIORENTINA

For an elegant vegetable to complete your Italian dinner menu, serve these artichoke bottoms and cauliflowerets with the creamy flavorful sauce in this recipe.

1 1/2 tbs. butter
3/4 cup mushrooms chopped
1/2 small onion, finely chopped
1/2 green pepper, finely minced
8 artichoke bottoms, cooked
1 cup, cooked firm cauliflowerets sauce

Sauté the mushrooms, onion, and green pepper in the hot butter until tender. Spoon equal amounts on each artichoke bottom. Place a few cauliflowerets on each artichoke and spoon a tablespoon of sauce over each. Serve immediately.

Sauce

2 tbs. butter
2 tbs. sifted flour
1/2 cup light cream
1/4 cup grated imported Swiss cheese
1/8 tsp. salt
white pepper and Dijon mustard to taste

Melt the butter in a pan. Add the flour, blending with a whisk until smooth, then add the cream, beating continuously until the sauce is thick and smooth. Add the cheese, whisking until fully incorporated into the sauce. Season lightly with salt, pepper, and mustard to give a nip to the sauce. Keep warm in a double boiler until ready to serve. Makes about one cup of sauce.

EGGPLANT FLORENTINE
MELANZANE FIORENTINA

Eggplant holds a prominent place in Italian cooking. It blends beautifully with capers, tomatoes, olives, mushrooms, anchovies, cheeses and is delicious fried, baked, sautéed, and roasted. This recipe combines it with cheese and bakes it to produce a creamy taste sensation.

2 medium peeled eggplants
salt
flour
1/2 cup olive oil2 1/2 cups tomato sauce (p.67)
1 lb. shredded mozzarella cheese
1 tbs. dried basil

Slice the eggplant 1/2" thick. Generously salt both sides of the eggplant slices and arrange them on several layers of paper towels. Place a pastry board over

them, weighted with large cans of juice or fruit, for 1 hour. Then thoroughly rinse the eggplant under cold running water and drain on paper towels. Pat completely dry.

Dust the eggplant with flour and sauté the slices in hot oil over high heat until brown. Layer the eggplant in an oiled 13" x 9" baking pan with the sauce, mozzarella cheese, and basil. There will be 3 layers. Reserve some of the cheese for a topping. Bake in a preheated 450° oven for 10 to 12 minutes until the dish is bubbly and the cheese slightly browned. Serves 6. Good by itself or with roasted meat or chicken. On occasion it is served as an appetizer.

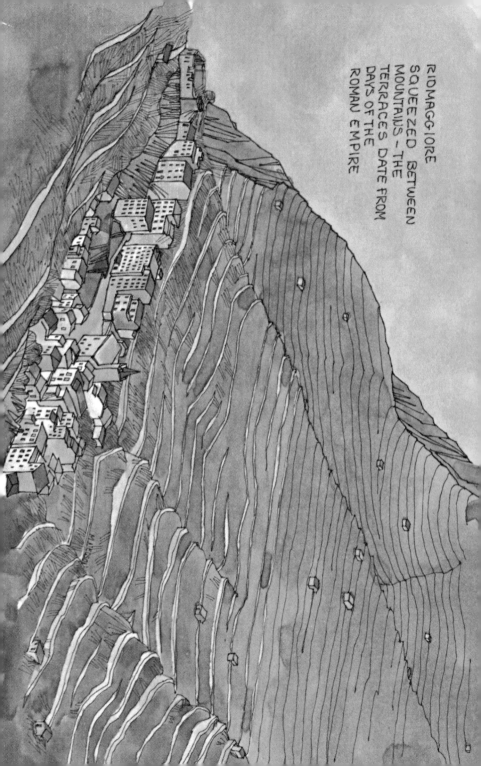

RIDMAGGIORE
SQUEEZED BETWEEN
MOUNTAINS - THE
TERRACES DATE FROM
DAYS OF THE
ROMAN EMPIRE

Pasta & Rice

The inventiveness and skill which Italians lavish on their pastas and the creation of pasta dishes is astounding. These foods are the staples of Italian cooking and can be served as a main dish or as a separate course in a main meal.

Italians are very proud of their pasta. Its quality must be of the highest. Sauces are used sparingly. You will never see the kind of sauce-drenched pasta that is served routinely in the United States. Pasta is always slightly chewy or al dente, as the Italians say. This applies to all pasta including such filled ones as tortellini and ravioli. Any resemblance to the real thing is coincidental! Once you have made your own pasta, you will be spoiled for life.

Rice dishes are quite delicate, frequently containing seafood. Each grain of rice should be separate—never mushy. Italian rice is longer grained than that grown in Texas or North Carolina and takes a slightly longer cooking time.

BASIC PASTA DOUGH
PASTA BASILARE

The majority of Italian cooks make their own pasta. Once you have tried it—you will see why. If your time is limited or if you insist on ready-made pastas, I suggest Italian, Chinese, or Manischewitz package noodles as the most authentic on the market. But try the do-it-yourself variety—it is easier than you think!

1 3/4 cups sifted flour
2 large eggs + 1 egg yolk
1 1/2 tsp. oil
1/2 tsp. salt

Trim an old clean sheet to generously cover your kitchen table or any other large flat surface and dust the sheet evenly with flour. This will keep the pasta from sticking to the cloth.

Place the flour in a large deep bowl. Beat together the remaining ingredients. Make a well in the flour and pour the liquid mixture into it. Mix the pasta with

your hand until everything is thoroughly blended, then knead it until the pasta is quite smooth. Rinse a clean linen towel in warm water and wring it out very well. Wrap the dough in the damp cloth and set aside for 30 minutes. Cover a pastry board with a floured pastry cloth. Use a floured stockinette cover for your rolling pin as this prevents the pasta from sticking to the board or the rolling pin. Place a piece of dough on the floured pastry cloth and roll it out until it is paper thin. If it will be larger than the board, cut it in half and roll each half separately so there are no thick edges. Place the rolled sheet of pasta on the floured sheet. Use the same procedure with the remaining dough. After all the dough has been used, lightly flour the surface of each sheet of pasta and roll it up into a tube. Cut the pasta into strips according to your taste, from 1/8" thick to 3" thick for lasagna. Uncoil these strips and place them back on the floured sheet to dry. After drying, they can be kept for a while in a cardboard box, a large cannister, or a plastic bag. This recipe makes about 3/4 pound of pasta and is the basic recipe for many other varieties of pasta, including ravioli.

NOODLES, VENETIAN STYLE
CHITARRATA ALLA MARINARA

Signor Michielotti of Ristorante Noemi in Venice prepared this delicacy for us at the table. It has the same theatrical appeal as Caesar salad or Crepes Suzette while remaining essentially simple to prepare.

The name Chitarrata refers to the way the pasta is formed. The pasta sheet is laid over a form containing 20 steel strings. A rolling pin rolled over the pasta cuts it and it drops under the strings. The resulting pasta is a very thin, flat noodle. If you are less ambitious, any good brand of egg noodle—the thin flat type—may be substituted.

1/4 lb. fatty bacon
1/3 lb. ham, finely diced
4 mussels, cooked and shelled
1/4 cup sweet red pepper, finely chopped
8 oz. hot cooked Chitarrata
cracked black pepper to taste

freshly grated Parmesan cheese
1 large fresh egg yolk
1/2 cup sweet butter in curls
soy sauce
2 tbs. green and black olives,
    finely chopped

Finely chop the bacon and sauté in a large heavy skillet over medium heat until some fat is released. Add the ham, mussels, and red pepper to the pan. Continue cooking until the ham is lightly browned and the pepper is tender. Keep warm. Add the remaining ingredients to the hot cooked pasta, one at a time, in this order: cracked pepper, grated Parmesan cheese, egg yolk, butter, soy sauce, the ham mixture, and the olives. Use a fork and spoon with a swirling motion to integrate each ingredient before adding the next one. Use a warm shallow bowl or a deep platter for a mixing container. Do not toss the ingredients because they will cool too rapidly. Serve additional grated Parmesan for sprinkling on each serving to taste. Serves 2. If you would like to serve this to more than 2 people, it is best to make 2 portions at a time rather than doubling the recipe.

MEAT SAUCE
RAGU

In Italy you are served just a little sauce on pasta, several tablespoons, instead of the wet, juicy pastas known here.

6 thick slices of bacon
1/4 lb. beef suet in thin slices
1 1/2 lbs. beef chuck with a bone
salt, freshly ground pepper to taste
1 split veal knuckle
3/4 lb. veal shank
1/4 lb. coarsely chopped mushrooms
2 peeled and chopped carrots
2 peeled and chopped onions
1/4 cup celery, mostly leaves

1 crumbled bay leaf
Italian herb blend to taste
1 crushed garlic clove
1/4 cup red wine
3 tsp. flour
3 tsp. olive oil
2 large ripe tomatoes,
 peeled, seeded, chopped
pinch sugar
2 qts. boiling beef stock

Blanch the bacon by placing it in a pot with 6 cups of cold water. Heat to boiling, simmer for 10 minutes, drain, and rinse under cold water. Pat dry on paper towels and set aside. Use the suet to line the bottom of a heavy 10-quart pot. Place the beef on the suet, season with salt and pepper, and lay the blanched bacon over the beef. Add the next 6 ingredients. Place uncovered in a preheated 450° oven for 15 to 20 minutes, turning the meat and bones occasionally so they will brown evenly. When the meat and bones have browned, remove them from the oven, add the bay leaf, herbs, garlic, and wine and cook over medium heat, uncovered, until there is almost no liquid left. Remove from the heat. Combine the flour and oil with a whisk into a smooth paste, add to the sauce, stir well, and replace the pot on the stove. Cook for 5 minutes, then add the tomato and sugar, stirring well. Add enough of the boiling stock to just cover the meat. Mix well and season to taste. Bring the sauce to a boil. Cover and bake in a preheated 300°oven for 4 to 5 hours. Remove from the oven, taking the meat and the bones out of the sauce. Line a strainer with clean cheesecloth or a clean HandiWipe. Pour the sauce

through the finest strainer. Pour the strained liquid into a smaller pot and cook over medium heat until the sauce is the consistency of tomato puree. Refrigerate overnight. Remove and discard the congealed fat. This sauce freezes well. Makes about 4 cups of sauce.

Save the meat from the veal shank in addition to the beef. Refrigerate and cut into tiny pieces when cold. Add to some of the sauce. Store separately. This can be used in Cannelloni Cremalati Roma (p.66), for example.

COCCONATO

STUFFED PASTA, MINERVETTA STYLE
CANNELLONI MINERVETTA

This dish is served at a restaurant overlooking the Bay of Naples. The food was as exquisite as the view.

Crepe Batter

3 large eggs
1/8 tsp. salt
1 1/2 cups light cream

1 1/8 cups sifted flour
2 tbs. corn oil
butter

Beat the eggs, salt, and cream together until foamy. Add the flour, whisk until smooth, then add the oil and refrigerate for 1 hour, during which time you can prepare the filling and topping. Pour 1 teaspoon oil into a seasoned black iron French crepe pan, No. 18. Add 1/2 teaspoon butter to the pan and place over medium-high heat. Wait until the fat sizzles, then ladle just enough batter into the pan so that the surface of the pan is barely covered when you rotate it. Replace

the pan over the heat until the top of the crepe appears "set", not liquid. On an electric range, rotate the pan several times for even heat. Do not turn the crepe. Remove to a foil-lined counter. Add another sliver of butter to the pan and repeat the procedure until no more batter remains. Makes 20 to 22 crepes. Keep them in a single layer—do not stack.

Cream Sauce

5 tbs. butter	freshly ground white pepper
4 tbs. flour	3 sprigs parsley
2 1/2 cups milk	1/4 tsp. powdered thyme
generous 1/2 tsp. salt	1 bay leaf

Use a heavy pot in which to melt the butter over medium heat. Add the flour and whisk to a smooth paste. Cook for a minute, then add the milk gradually,

stirring with a whisk, to form a smooth mixture. Season to taste with the salt and pepper, then add the parsley, thyme, and bay leaf. Cook the sauce over medium heat, stirring constantly with the whisk until it comes to a boil. Lower the heat and simmer for 10 to 15 minutes longer, continuing to stir. Pour the sauce through a strainer into a large heavy-bottomed pot.

Filling
1 lb. diced mozzarella cheese
1/4 lb. chopped mild ham (Prague)
Cream Sauce (p.62)
5 large egg yolks

Topping
1/2 lb. sliced fresh mushrooms
1/4 cup butter
1 1/2 cups Meat Sauce (p.58)
freshly grated Parmesan cheese

Add the cheese and ham to the Cream Sauce, mixing thoroughly. Cool. Add the egg yolks, stirring well with the whisk, and cook over the lowest heat for about 10 minutes, stirring continuously with the whisk. Let cool for a few

minutes.

Spoon about 3 tablespoons of filling down the center of the browned side of each crepe. Roll and place in two well-greased 13" x 9" pans. At this point you can refrigerate the cannelloni, covered, for several hours if you wish. Sauté the mushrooms in the butter. Spoon them over the top of the cannelloni in both pans. Drizzle the Meat Sauce equally over both pans of cannelloni. Bake in a preheated 375° oven for 15 to 20 minutes until completely hot. If it has been refrigerated, heat for 30 to 40 minutes. Sprinkle a little Parmesan cheese over them just before serving and have a bowl of grated Parmesan on the table. Makes about 20 to 22 cannelloni. Serves 6 to 8.

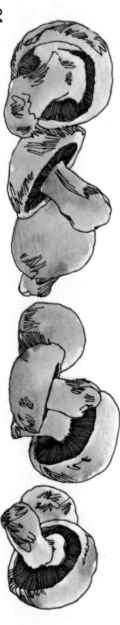

THE PIETÀ - COMPLETED
BY MICHELANGELO WHEN
HE WAS 24 YEARS OLD.

IN THE
CHAPEL OF THE PIETÀ,
THE VATICAN - ROME

STUFFED PASTA, ROMAN STYLE
CANNELLONI ROMANA

This recipe is almost an inside out Roman version of Cannelloni Minervetta.

1 recipe crepes (p.61)
3 1/2 cups Meat Sauce (p.58)
6 to 8 large peeled, seeded, ripe tomatoes

2 tbs. butter
freshly grated Parmesan cheese

Prepare the crepes from recipe on page 61. Dice the meat from the Meat Sauce, replace it in the sauce, and refrigerate. It is easier to use if cold. Spoon 2 to 3 tablespoons of sauce down the center of each crepe on the browned side. Roll up and place side by side in two well-greased 13" x 9" pans. Cut the tomatoes into thin strips and lightly sauté until limp. Spoon the tomatoes evenly over the cannelloni. Bake in a preheated 375° oven for 25 to 35 minutes, until piping hot. If they appear to be browning too rapidly, lightly cover the top of each pan with a sheet of aluminum foil. Serves 6 to 8. Pass the grated Parmesan cheese at the table.

TOMATO SAUCE
SALSA AL POMODORO

1 small onion, finely minced
2 tbs. olive oil
1/4 cup diced ham
1 tbs. flour
1 bay leaf
salt
sugar

freshly ground pepper
Italian herb blend to taste
3 1/2 cups canned Italian plum
    tomatoes or 6 large ripe tomatoes,
    peeled, seeded, and chopped

Sauté the onion in oil over medium heat. Add the ham, cooking until both are browned. Sprinkle the flour evenly over the ham-onion mixture, mixing well. Lower the heat slightly and add the remaining ingredients. Simmer for an hour, stirring occasionally, then strain through a sieve lined with clean cheesecloth. Makes about 3 cups. Freezes well. Try freezing it in a plastic ice cube tray. Unlike the American concept, very little sauce should be served on pastas. One cube is ample for 2 to 3 portions.

GREEN PASTA
PASTA VERDE

1 10-oz. pkg. frozen chopped spinach
2 large eggs
1 tbs. oil

1 tsp. salt
3 1/4 cups flour

Cook spinach, cool, and wring out excess moisture. Puree in the blender. Beat together eggs, oil and salt. Put the flour into a large bowl and make a well in the center. Pour the eggs and the spinach into the well. Knead thoroughly until smooth. Wrap the dough in a damp linen cloth then let it rest for 30 minutes. Divide the dough into 4 parts. Roll one part out on a well-floured pastry cloth using a stockinette cover for the rolling pin. The lasagna should be about 1/8" thick. Transfer to a lightly floured piece of waxed paper and roll out the remaining pieces of dough. Place one piece of pasta back on the board and cut into 3" wide strips or squares. Spread on a lightly floured sheet to dry. Repeat with remaining dough. Make the pasta the day before you assemble the dish so it has time to dry.

GREEN LASAGNA, RAVENNA STYLE
LASAGNA VERDE ALLA RAVENNA

1 1/2 cups Cream Sauce (p.62)
2 1/2 cups Sauce Bolognese (p.70)
1 cup freshly grated Parmesan cheese
1/4 cup melted sweet butter

Cook green pasta in 4 quarts of boiling salted water until just tender. Add 2 cups cold water to stop the cooking process and remove from the heat. Remove the pasta from the pot using a slotted spoon. Lay the noodles in a single layer on a cloth that has been dipped in warm water and thoroughly wrung out. Butter a 13" x 9" baking pan and line the bottom with a single layer of pasta. Spread a little cream sauce on the pasta, then some Sauce Bolognese, and finally, some grated Parmesan cheese. Repeat the layers, ending with a layer of pasta. Sprinkle remaining Parmesan cheese over the top, drizzle with melted butter and bake in a preheated 350° oven for 30 to 45 minutes. Serves 6 to 8.

BOLOGNESE SAUCE
SALSA BOLOGNESE

1/4 cup olive oil
1 medium chopped onion
3 crushed cloves garlic
2 peeled and finely chopped carrots
3 chopped celery stalks
6 oz. chopped smoked ham
1/2 lb. very lean ground beef

1/2 cup dry Marsala or sherry (wine)
1 six. oz. can tomato paste
2 1/2 cups canned Italian plum tomatoes
    packed in tomato puree
sugar
salt and freshly ground pepper
Italian herb blend to taste

Heat the oil in a large, heavy-bottomed skillet. Saute the onion, garlic, carrots, celery, and ham until the vegetables are tender and the ham lightly browned. Add the ground beef, tossing until it loses its redness. Add the wine, stirring well to loosen the well-browned particles from the bottom of the pan, and simmer for several minutes. Add the remaining ingredients, mixing well, and continue to simmer, uncovered, for 2 1/2 to 3 hours. Adjust the seasoning. Makes 3 to 4 cups of sauce. Freezes well.

SPAGHETTI, CARBONARA STYLE
SPAGHETTI ALLA CARBONARA

1/4 lb. salt pork
1 lb. spaghetti
1 tbs. olive oil
4 large fresh eggs
3/4 cup freshly grated Parmesan cheese

1/4 cup heavy cream
salt
freshly ground pepper to taste
1/4 cup sweet butter

Blanch the salt pork by placing it in a pot containing 6 cups of cold water. Bring to a boil, simmer for 10 minutes, drain, rinse under cold water, and pat dry on paper towels. Cut into small dice and saute over high heat until crisp and well browned. Drain and blot excess fat on paper towels. Cook the spaghetti in a generous amount of boiling salted water just until tender. Meanwhile whisk together the eggs, cheese, and cream. Melt the butter, and continue heating until it is lightly browned. The spaghetti should be done and drained at this point. Whisk the egg mixture in the butter. As it thickens add the salt pork and spaghetti and serve immediately. Ample for 6.

SPICY PASTA
RIGATONI ALL' ARRABBIATA

This spicy pasta dish can be served in small bowls as the pasta course of an Italian dinner.

3/4 cup Tomato Sauce (p.67)
tabasco sauce to taste
Worcestershire Sauce to taste
12 oz. Rigatoni cooked al dente
1/4 cup butter

Simmer the tomato sauce until piping hot. Add enough tabasco sauce and Worcestershire Sauce until the mixture has a real "bite." Simmer for another 15 to 20 minutes. Toss the hot Rigatoni with butter until evenly coated. Serve the pasta in warm shallow soup bowls, placing 2 teaspoons of sauce in the center of each bowl. Have salt and pepper grinders at the table. Serves 6.

MACARONI, POLI STYLE
MACCHERONI ALLA POLI

A Venetian pasta with seafood sauce, a specialty of Signor Poli, Ristorante Peoceto Risorto.

2 tbs. sweet butter
1 tbs. grated onion
1 small crushed clove of garlic
1/2 lb. fresh sliced mushrooms
1 10-oz. pkg. frozen petit pois (tiny peas)
1 large ripe tomato, peeled, seeded and diced
1 cup tiny cooked shrimp

1 small can tuna fish, drained
salt and freshly ground pepper
nutmeg to taste
8 oz. hot cooked macaroni
freshly grated Parmesan cheese
freshly grated Pecorino cheese

Sauté the onion, garlic, and mushrooms until tender. Add the peas, the tomato, and cook uncovered until they are tender. Add the seafood and continue to simmer for 5 minutes. Season with salt, pepper, a pinch of nutmeg, and serve in warm, shallow soup bowls with several tablespoons of sauce in the center of the pasta. Sprinkle with grated cheeses. Serves 6.

73

RICE, VENETIAN STYLE
RISOTTO ALLA VENEZIANA

This delightful seafood dish is delicate, creamy and unique.

1 lb. uncooked medium shrimp
2 cups dry white wine
1 stalk celery, cut into small pieces
1/4 cup parsley
12 steamed shelled mussels
3 tbs. butter
2 cups Italian or long grained white rice
salt, freshly ground white pepper to taste
clam juice
2 egg yolks
1/4 cup butter
1/4 cup parsley, finely minced

Wash the shrimp and place them in a heavy pot. Add the wine, celery, parsley, and enough water to completely cover the shrimp. Cover, bring to a boil, then lower the heat and simmer just until the shrimp turn pink. Remove from the heat, drain, and reserve the broth. Shell the shrimp, devein them, and return the shells to the broth. Bring to a boil, lower the heat, and simmer for 15 to 20 minutes. There should be at least 1 cup of broth remaining. Pour the broth through a strainer lined with clean cheesecloth. Meanwhile coarsely chop the shrimp and reserve with the mussels. Melt the butter over medium heat in a heavy-bottomed pot. Add the rice and stir for several minutes, then add the broth and season very lightly. Bring to a boil, lower the heat slightly, and add enough clam juice from time to time to keep the rice moist. It will take about 20 minutes until it is just tender, not mushy. Gently stir in the seafood and remove from the heat. Add the egg yolks, mixing well, and the butter. Serve on a hot platter using parsley as a garnish. Serves 6 generously.

PONTE VECCHIO
AN ANCIENT
COVERED BRIDGE
FLORENCE

SHRIMP AND RICE
RISOTTO CON SCAMPI

This recipe is delicious as a separate course or it may be served as an entree followed by a salad.

3 tbs. butter
2 cups Italian or long grain rice
Sauce (p.78)

3 cups water
1 tsp. salt
1 tsp. lemon juice

Melt butter in a heavy pot. Add rice and stir until coated with butter but not browned, then add the remaining ingredients except the sauce. Bring to a boil, stir with a fork, cover, and reduce the heat to the lowest setting. Leave over low heat for 15 to 20 minutes and do not uncover or stir during this time. Stir with a fork just before serving. Place the rice on one half of a clean, starched, white linen napkin. Fold the napkin to enclose the rice, and place it on a hot platter. Serve the sauce separately in a hot bowl.

Sauce

1 lb. cooked medium shrimp
and broth (p.74)

3 tbs. butter

3 tbs. flour

1 cup shrimp broth (p.74)

2 cups light cream or half and half

salt

freshly ground white pepper to taste

Prepare the shrimp and broth. Melt the butter over medium heat in a large skillet. Sprinkle the flour over the butter, using a whisk to make a smooth paste. Add broth and cream, stirring continuously with the whisk until smooth. When sauce has thickened, season very delicately to taste, add the shrimp, and serve in a warm bowl. Ladle generous portions of sauce over each serving of rice. This is served as a course by itself with nothing else on the plate.

TO SHAPE RAVIOLI

The simplest way to shape ravioli is to spread half the filling evenly on 1 sheet of pasta. Cover with another sheet and roll with a special wooden ravioli pin, pressing firmly to shape and seal the ravioli. Cut along the divisions with a fluted pastry wheel.

Or you can place small mounds of filling about 2″ apart on one sheet of pasta. Cover with another sheet of pasta and form by using a square ravioli stamp. The stamp both seals and cuts the ravioli. You may also form the ravioli by sealing them with the side of your hand.

Note that homemade ravioli has some firmness to it. It in no way resembles or should resemble the soft ravioli sold in cans. It should be al dente.

GREEN RAVIOLINI, GOBBI STYLE
RAVIOLINI VERDE ALLA GOBBI

For this Florentine recipe, we shape the raviolini like Chinese won ton.

Green Pasta (p.68)
3 10-oz. pkgs. frozen chopped spinach
1 1/2 cups sieved ricotta cheese
1 tbs. sweet butter at room temperature

3 large egg yolks
1/2 cup freshly grated Parmesan cheese
1 tsp. salt
freshly ground pepper to taste

Prepare the dough as directed on page 68. Let it rest while you prepare the filling. Cook the spinach, drain, cook, and squeeze out all excess moisture with your hands. Puree the spinach in the blender then mix with the remaining ingredients.

Divide the dough into 4 equal parts. Roll out 1 piece into a very thin sheet and cut into 2" squares. Put 1/2 teaspoon of filling in the center of each square. Holding the dough with both hands, fingers underneath and thumb on the top, fold each side toward the center and overlap. Press the seam together with your

thumbs. Fold in half again with the filling in the center. Two tabs have been formed, one on each side of the filling. Fold the tabs backwards, moisten the corner of each one, and press together firmly using a thumb and forefinger. Set the completed raviolini on a floured sheet and repeat with the remaining dough. Cook in 5 or 6 batches in a large pot of boiling salted water for 8 to 10 minutes. Remove with a slotted spoon and place in a heavy serving bowl with generous lumps of butter. Serve with grated Parmesan.

If you do not wish to serve the raviolini all at once, you can freeze them. First place them on a floured cookie sheet. Dust lightly with flour and freeze. When they are firm, place them in layers in a foil pan. Keep a sheet of foil between the layers. They are delicate so do not omit the first step when freezing them. Thaw before cooking.

RAVIOLI, HOUSE STYLE
RAVIOLI ALLA MODA DI CASA

2 cups fresh ricotta cheese
4 egg yolks
1/4 cup grated Parmesan cheese
1 tsp. salt

freshly ground pepper to taste
Pasta dough (p.54)
3/4 cup sweet butter
1 1/2 cups freshly grated Parmesan cheese

Press the ricotta through a sieve using a wooden spoon. Mix well with the egg yolks, Parmesan cheese, salt, pepper, and set aside.

Prepare the pasta dough. Divide it into 4 equal parts and roll out 1 piece of dough as thinly as possible on a floured pastry cloth. Use a floured stockinette cover for the rolling pin. Lay this sheet of dough on a floured cloth and roll out a second piece of dough. Form as directed on page 79. Place the finished ravioli on a floured sheet spread on the kitchen table. Let them dry for a while—2 to 3 hours should be sufficient. Now they can be frozen on a floured foil-lined cookie sheet. Dust the tops of the ravioli with more flour and freeze. Once they are firm, the ravioli can be layered in square foil pans. Keep a sheet of foil between the

layers. Enclose the pans in plastic bags and tie shut.

To cook: Drop a few ravioli at a time into a large pot of boiling salted water. Cook for about 8 to 10 minutes. Remove with a slotted spoon and drain on linen towels. Put the ravioli in a warm serving dish with slices of butter between the layers. Sprinkle with Parmesan and serve with additional Parmesan cheese at the table. Serves 6.

Variation

Serve the Ricotta-filled ravioli with 1 1/2 cups hot tomato sauce (p.67), reducing the butter to 1/4 cup. Serve in individual warmed shallow soup bowls with 2 tablespoons of sauce spooned into the center of each serving. Pass additional sauce at the table with the Parmesan cheese.

CORNMEAL MUSH
POLENTA

Polenta is often served in the place of rice or pasta.

4 cups water
2 tsp. salt
1 cup polenta or white or yellow cornmeal (waterground variety is best)

Bring the water and salt to a rolling boil using the top part of a double boiler over direct heat. Add the cornmeal in a slow stream, stirring constantly with a whisk. Cook until it begins to thicken, then place the pan over the bottom part of the double boiler which holds boiling water. Cook for 40 to 50 minutes, stirring from time to time. Wet the inside of a 9" x 5" loaf pan. Shake the excess water out. Spread the hot polenta in the loaf pan, smoothing the top to an even surface. Refrigerate until cold. To serve, slice the polenta 1/4" to 1/2" thick. Sauté on both sides in butter until golden brown. Or deep-fry the slices at 375° until golden brown. Can also be served with a meat sauce.

HERB SAUCE, GENOA STYLE
PESTO GENOVESE

To obtain the same fresh herb flavor we experienced in Italy, you should grow your own fresh basil on the windowsill in the kitchen.

1 cup fresh basil leaves
2 crushed garlic cloves
1/4 cup olive oil
3 tbs. pine nuts

1 1/2 tbs. water
2 tbs. grated Romano cheese
2 tbs. grated Parmesan cheese

Put the basil, garlic, oil, nuts, and water in the blender. Mix at low speed for about 1 minute. Add the cheeses. Mix on low speed for 1/2 minute and then at high speed for another 1/2 minute. This must be served immediately or it will discolor. Makes approximately 3/4 cup. It can be frozen but must be kept covered until it has thawed. As soon as the air hits it, the pesto darkens.

SPAGHETTI WITH HERB SAUCE, GENOA STYLE
SPAGHETTI CON PESTO GENOVESE

Here is a deliciously different way to serve spaghetti.

1 lb. spaghetti
Pesto Genovese (p.85)
1/2 cup butter at room temperature
2 cups freshly grated Parmesan cheese

Cook the spaghetti in 6 quarts of boiling salted water until barely tender. As soon as this point is reached, pour 2 cups of cold water into the pot to stop the cooking process. Drain well and, using a fork and a soup spoon, swirl in a large warmed bowl with the Pesto and butter. Add the cheese and swirl again. Serve immediately with more Parmesan cheese on the table. Serves 8 to 10. Be sure to serve on warmed plates.

NOODLES WITH HERB SAUCE, GENOA STYLE
FETTUCCINO CON PESTO GENOVESE

Serve this fettuccine as a separate course or as an accompaniment for grilled meat or fish.

1 recipe Pasta (p.54)
4 large peeled potatoes

1/4 cup EACH grated Parmesan and Pecorino cheeses
Double recipe Pesto Genovese (p.85)

Roll the pasta very thin on a floured pastry cloth. Keeping the dough well floured, roll it up loosely and slice about 1/4" thick. Uncoil the fettuccine on a lightly floured sheet placed on a large flat surface and dry for an hour or so.

Thinly slice the potatoes. Place in a large pot filled with cold salted water, bring to a boil, reduce the heat to medium, and cook for 10 minutes. Increase heat, add the fettuccine, and cook until just al dente. Drain the fettuccine and potatoes, reserving 1/4 cup of the cooking liquid. Put the potatoes and fettuccine in a hot shallow bowl, and sprinkle with cheese and cooking broth. Gently swirl to mix and serve immediately. Serves 6.

ENGLISH RICE
RISO ALL'INGLESE

This is a standard Italian accompaniment to almost any main dish.

1/2 cup sweet butter
1 1/4 cups raw long grain white rice or Italian rice
2 cups boiling chicken stock, beef stock, or clam juice
pinch of salt

Melt the butter over medium heat in a medium-sized skillet. Add the rice, tossing to coat evenly with the butter, but do not brown. Add the boiling stock and salt. Stir well with a fork, then reduce the heat to the lowest setting. Cover and cook for 25 to 30 minutes until all the liquid has been absorbed. Each grain of rice will be separate yet cooked. Add the remaining butter, stir with a fork, and serve in a warm bowl. Serves 6.

NOTE: Use the stock most suitable for the rest of the meal—beef with beef or lamb; chicken with veal, chicken or ham; and clam juice with seafood.

A FIORAIA READIES HER FLOWERS
FOR THE DAYS SALES ~ NAPLES

POTATO GNOCCHI WITH MEAT SAUCE
GNOCCHI DI PATATE AL SUGO DI CARNE

The correct pronunciation is "Nyawky."

4 cups warm mashed potatoes

2 cups flour (unsifted)

2 tsp. salt

2 large eggs + 1 egg yolk

4 tsp. olive oil

1/4 cup butter

1 1/2 cups Sauce Bolognese (p.70)

1 1/4 cups freshly grated Parmesan cheese

Using a fork, combine the potatoes, flour, and salt. Beat the eggs and oil together. Add to the potatoes, mix well, then knead until smooth on a floured pastry board. Divide the dough into 6 to 8 pieces. Generously dust your hands with flour and roll a piece of dough back and forth under your hands forming a

rope about 1/2″ in diameter. Cut into pieces 1″ long, pinching each piece in the center lightly with your forefinger. It will resemble a bowtie.

Line up the gnocchi on a well-floured sheet covering the kitchen table. Do not let the gnocchi touch each other. Form the rest of the dough into gnocchi, placing them all on the floured sheet. Bring a large pot of salted water to a rolling boil. Drop a few gnocchi at a time into the pot, keeping the water at a gentle boil. Cook them for 5 minutes. Remove from the pot with a slotted spoon, drain well, and keep warm in a covered, buttered, shallow dish in a 150° oven. Continue cooking the gnocchi until all have been cooked. Add the butter to the gnocchi, stirring gently. Heat the Sauce Bolognese. Serve gnocchi in warm shallow soup bowls, spooning 2 tablespoons of sauce into the center of each serving. Pass a bowl of Parmesan cheese at the table. Serves 6 as a main dish and 10 as a pasta course.

GREEN DUMPLINGS
GNOCCHI VERDE, ANTICO FALCONE

These gnocchi are delicate, fluffy, incredibly light—and habit-forming!

3 10-oz. pkgs. frozen chopped spinach
6 tbs. butter
1 1/8 cups fresh ricotta cheese
3 large beaten eggs
1/2 cup + 1 tbs. flour
3/8 cup freshly grated Parmesan cheese
3/4 tsp. salt
freshly ground pepper to taste
3/4 cup freshly grated Parmesan cheese

Thaw the spinach, place it in a linen towel, and squeeze out all the excess moisture. Finely mince the spinach. Melt the butter over medium heat in a large heavy skillet and add the spinach, stirring for several minutes. When the spinach

becomes very dry, add the ricotta. Cook, stirring constantly, for several minutes. Turn the spinach-cheese mixture into a large bowl and add the eggs, flour, grated cheese, salt, and pepper, mixing well. Cover and refrigerate for 1 hour until the mixture is firm enough to handle.

Bring 4 quarts of salted water to a boil. Lower the heat to medium. Dust your hands with flour. Shape a tablespoon or less of dough into a ball no larger than 1 1/2″ in diameter. Gently drop the balls into the water. Simmer uncovered for 6 to 8 minutes. They expand a bit and have the consistency of a tender matzo ball, spongy and light. Using a slotted spoon, remove the cooked gnocchi from the water and drain well on a linen towel. Continue to form gnocchi and cook them until all the batter has been used. Place the gnocchi in warm shallow soup bowls. Drizzle them with melted butter and sprinkle with grated Parmesan cheese. Serve immediately. Pass more Parmesan cheese at the table. Serves 6 to 8.

TWISTED PASTA
TORTELLINI

These tortellini are also delicious served in a strong beef or chicken stock.

1/2 lb. cooked chicken breasts
1/2 lb. mild ham
2 tbs. grated Parmesan
freshly ground pepper

nutmeg to taste
2 large egg yolks
Pasta dough (p.54)

Remove the skin from the chicken. Take all the meat from the bones in as large pieces as possible. Using the finest blade of the grinder, grind the chicken and ham. Add the remaining ingredients except for the pasta, mixing to a smooth paste. Set aside.

Divide the pasta dough into 4 parts. Roll 1 piece of dough as thin as possible. Using a 1 1/2" fluted cookie cutter, cut into circles 1 1/2" in diameter. Put about 1/2 teaspoon of filling, shaped into a ball, in the center of each pasta circle. Slightly dampen the edges of the circles and fold in half, forming a half-moon.

You can use a fork to seal the seam securely. As you make the half-moons, place them on a lightly floured sheet. Repeat with the remaining dough and filling. Let them dry for an hour or two. To freeze the tortellini, lay them in a single layer on a cookie sheet lined with a lightly floured sheet of foil. Do not let the tortellini touch each other. Freeze until firm, then layer the tortellini in pans with a sheet of foil between each layer. Enclose the pan in a plastic bag and tie shut.

To cook: Drop the tortellini, a few at a time, into 4 quarts of boiling salted water. Cook for 10 to 15 minutes. Remove from the water with a slotted spoon and drain on a linen towel. Serve in chicken or beef stock, place in hot, shallow soup bowls, drizzle with 1/4 cup melted butter and serve with grated Pecorino cheese.

Or, after drizzling with the melted butter, spoon 2 tablespoons of hot Sauce Bolognese (p.70) in the center of each serving. Use a total of 3/4 cup of Sauce Bolognese. Serve with 1 1/4 cups grated Pecorino cheese at the table. Serves 6.

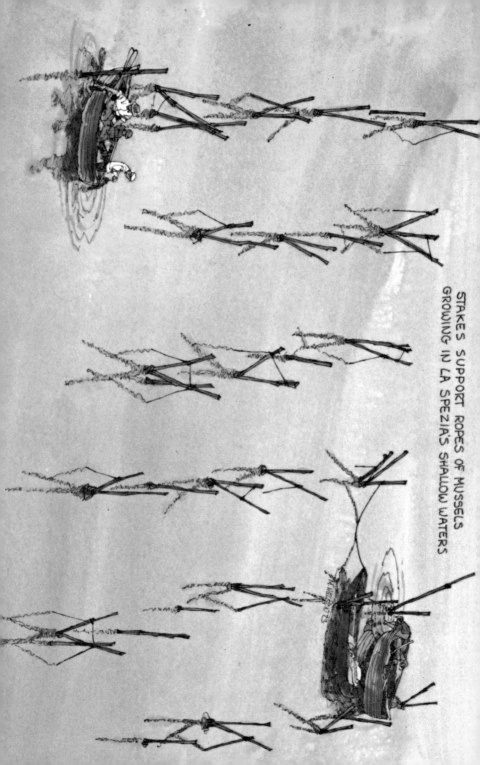

STAKES SUPPORT ROPES OF MUSSELS
GROWING IN LA SPEZIA'S SHALLOW WATERS

Meats & Fish

Meat is plentiful and good in Italy and any and all cuts of beef are pampered into succulence by the Italian chef. Milk-fed veal, much of it from Lombardy, is featured in a great many dishes. The thin slice of veal, often pounded thinner, is the basic theme on which many chefs build their subtle variations. Lamb can be exceptionally tasty and uniquely Italian when dressed up with garlic, rosemary, truffles, or anchovies and red wine.

Modern Italians are fond of pork and, in addition to the roasts, chops, and ribs, they make a number of good pork sausages. Usually they prefer fresh lemon with pork instead of the applesauce favored in America. Variety cuts are widely used in Italian kitchens and many recipes are available featuring these variety meats.

Chicken has numerous variations—broiled, pan-fried, oven-baked, grilled, stuffed, (not with bread, but with ham, chestnuts, sausage, olives, etc.!) or smothered in mushrooms, ham, and melted cheese.

The seafood in Italy is justly famous and a glance at a map of this country reveals why fish is abundantly displayed in the markets. Since they are almost entirely surrounded by water, virtually every kind of fish and shellfish has appeared on Italian tables from the time of the early Romans.

Italian meals are robust and the main course reflects this. A national favorite, such as Bolliti Misti, is the Italian version of a boiled dinner and, prepared with care, is a gourmet treat. It is served with Salsa Verde, a combination sauce-dressing, which complements the assorted meats and vegetables and gives the dish its special Italian flavor.

Included here are such Venetian specialties as Osei Scampai, a brochette of assorted meats and vegetables which can be grilled outside. It represents the simpler side of Italian cuisine and, typically, it is served with polenta.

These recipes are easy to prepare and rewarding, both in palate-pleasing results and in compliments to the cook. They are commonly found on menus throughout Italy but rarely prepared or served here. It is time for a change!

STEAK, FLORENTINE STYLE
BISTECCHE ALLA FIORENTINA

The secret of the fantastic flavor of this renowned Florentine specialty is quite simple. A good restaurateur does not keep sliced steaks ready to fill the order. He slices them as they are ordered. They are juicier and more flavorful.

1/2 small clove of garlic, finely minced
2 tsp. finely minced parsley
olive oil
1 T-bone steak cut 1'' to 1 1/4'' thick
2 lemon wedges

Mix the garlic and parsley with just enough oil to make a paste. Pat this on both sides of the steak and leave at room temperature for 20 minutes. Broil close to the flame or grill over gas or charcoal, about 6 minutes on each side for medium rare. Pour about 1 teaspoon olive oil on a warmed plate. Place the steak on this and serve immediately, garnished with lemon wedges. Serves 1.

BROCHETTES OF MIXED MEATS
OSEI SCAMPAI

Scampai is Venetian argot meaning "cooked like a bird."

1 1/2 lbs. pork filet
1 1/2 lbs. boneless veal from the leg
12 chicken livers
3 mild Italian sausages
24 large mushroom caps
flour
fresh sage leaves or powdered sage to taste
1/4 cup melted butter
white wine
6-1/4" thick slices of cold Polenta (p.76)

Cut the pork and veal 1/4" thick and into 2" squares. Remove membranes and fat from the chicken livers, rinse the livers, and pat dry. Simmer the sausages

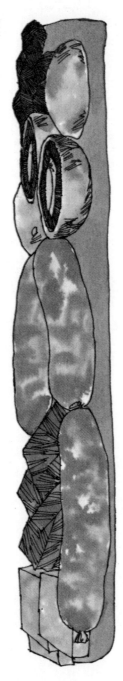

in water to cover for 20 minutes then drain on paper towels. Cool and cut each sausage into 6 pieces. Wash the mushroom caps and pat dry.

Using 6 small skewers, alternate the meats and sausage with the mushroom caps. If you have fresh leaf sage, insert it in several places on the skewer. Otherwise season the meats with salt, pepper, and powdered sage. Dust on all sides with flour and grill over charcoal, a gas grill, or in a broiler. Baste alternately with melted butter and wine. It should take about 5 minutes on each side.

Meanwhile sauté the polenta slices in butter until golden brown. Place each polenta slice on a warmed plate and place a skewer of grilled meat on it. Each person removes the meats from his own skewer. Serves 6.

BROCHETTE OF MIXED MEATS NO. 2
OSEI SCAMPAI II

1/2 lb. fatty bacon in 1 piece

1 1/2 lbs. pork filet

1 1/2 lbs. beef filet

1/2 lb. beef liver cut
    into 1/2" thick slices

24 tiny roasted cooled
    potato balls (p.115)

fresh rosemary leaves or dried rosemary

24 bay leaves

olive oil

6 slices Polenta cut 1/2" thick (p. 84)

3 tbs. butter

Cut the bacon and pork into 1/4" thick slices. Slice the beef 1/2" thick. Then cut all the meats into 1" x 2" pieces. Thread the meats and potatoes alternately on 12 six-inch wooden skewers. Season with rosemary and impale a bay leaf on each end of all the skewers. Brush with olive oil and broil or grill for about 15 minutes, turning to cook both sides. Baste every 5 minutes with oil. Meanwhile, sauté the polenta in hot butter until golden brown. Lay the skewers of cooked meats on the polenta. Serves 6.

BRAISED BEEF IN SAUCE WITH CORNMEAL MUSH
STRACOTTA HERBE, POLENTA

suet
5 lb. boneless rump roast
salt
freshly ground pepper to taste

onion powder to taste
2/3 cup water
1 1/2 cups Sauce Bolognese (p.70)

Render about 3 tablespoons fat from the suet in a heavy-bottomed pan. Remove the remaining suet from the pot. Pat the roast dry on paper towels. Over medium high heat, brown the roast on all sides in the fat, seasoning the meat with the salt, pepper and onion powder as you turn it. After the meat is well-browned, add the water, cover, and simmer for 3 hours or until tender. Cool and cut against the grain into slices about 1/4" thick. About 45 minutes before serving, layer the sliced meat in a shallow casserole. Cover with the Sauce Bolognese that has been mixed with the pan juices from the roast. Heat, covered, in a preheated 350° oven for 30 to 40 minutes. Serve with grilled slices of polenta. Makes 8 to 10 servings.

ITALIAN BOILED DINNER
BOLLITO MISTO

Bolliti Misti is a specialty of the northern city of Bergamo and is popular all over Italy.

2 lbs. very lean beef short ribs
4 lbs. beef rump
4 to 6 marrow bones
4 spicy Italian sausages
1 1/2 lbs. breast of veal
1 lb. breast of lamb
1 calves foot
1/2 lb. blanched lean salt pork
Select 1 lb. EACH of 6 of the following vegetables: broccoli, peas, green beans, cauliflower, mushrooms, cabbage, leeks, zucchini, carrots, Brussel sprouts
1 lb. cooked new potatoes
12 small cooked white onions

1 large peeled onion
2 cloves of garlic, peeled
2 peeled sliced carrots
3 large, ripe, peeled, seeded, chopped tomatoes
1/2 tsp. dried Bouquet Garni
1 bay leaf
salt
freshly ground pepper to taste

8 cups Chicken Stock (p.22)
3 cups Salsa Verda (p.106)

Put all the meats and bones into a very large heavy-bottomed pot. Pour in more than enough water to completely cover the contents. Slowly bring to a boil. Remove any scum on the top and reduce the heat to low. Add the onion, garlic, carrots, tomatoes, Bouquet Garni, and bay leaf. Season with salt and pepper and simmer for 1 1/2 to 2 hours. Remove the veal and lamb as soon as they are done, taking out the sausages at the same time. Place the cooked meats in a small pot with some broth to keep them moist, cover, and keep warm (perhaps on an electric hottray). Continue to simmer the remaining meat until it is tender, 1 to 1 1/2 hours. About 30 minutes before the beef will be done, cook the 6 fresh vegetables in chicken stock, using a separate pan. When they are cooked, drain and keep them warm in a 250° oven. Reheat the potatoes and onions in the oven for about 20 to 25 minutes in some broth. When the beef is done, arrange all the meats on a large platter with the drained cooked vegetables on another large warm platter. The Salsa Verde (p.106) is served with this at the table. Serves 8 to 10 generously.

GREEN SAUCE
SALSA VERDE

1 bunch parsley
3 anchovy fillets
1 cold cooked peeled potato
1 peeled clove of garlic
1 small peeled white onion

salt
freshly ground pepper to taste
1/4 cup well-drained capers
1 cup olive oil
2 tbs. white wine vinegar

Wash parsley thoroughly, remove and discard all stems. Squeeze the parsley to remove excess water, mince finely and place in a bowl. Rinse the anchovies in cold running water to rid them of their salty taste. Finely mince the anchovies, potato, garlic, and onion. Add the parsley, season, and mix well. Beat in the oil, a little at a time and, finally, the vinegar. Serve at room temperature. Makes about 1 3/4 cups.

LIVER, VENETIAN STYLE
FEGATO ALLA VENEZIANA

Even the most confirmed liver hater will have to give this the nod.

2 lbs. calves liver, sliced 1/4" thick
salt
freshly ground pepper to taste
flour
1/3 cup olive oil

3 tbs. butter
2 thinly-sliced peeled onions
1/3 cup white wine vinegar
4 lemons, quartered

Cut the liver into 1" x 2" strips. Season with salt and pepper and lightly dredge with flour. Heat the oil and butter over high heat, and sauté strips very quickly—just until they lose their raw look. Remove liver to a warm platter and place in a 200° oven. Put the onions in the hot butter/oil and sauté until they are golden. Add the vinegar and cook over high heat for several minutes to reduce the juices. Spoon the onions and pan juices over the liver on the platter and garnish with lemon wedges. Serves 6 to 8.

VEAL CHOPS WITH MUSHROOMS
COSTOLETTE DI VITELLO CON FUNGHI

6 rib veal chops cut 1" thick
salt and freshly ground pepper to taste
flour
2 large beaten eggs

6 tbs. butter
3 tbs. warmed cognac
1 lb. fresh sliced mushrooms
1/4 cup butter

Lightly season the chops, sprinkle them with flour, and shake off the excess. Dip the chops into the egg, then into the flour, and lay them on a rack until all the chops have been coated. Using a large heavy skillet, melt the butter over medium-high heat and sauté several chops at a time on both sides until nicely browned. It takes less than 5 minutes on each side. When they are all browned, add the cognac to the drippings. Flame it. Replace the chops in the skillet, overlapping to fit them all in. Lower the heat, cover, and simmer for 10 minutes. Turn the chops, baste with the pan juices, and cook about 10 minutes longer. Meanwhile sauté the mushrooms in butter until tender. Serve the chops on warmed plates with sautéed mushrooms over each chop. Serves 6.

A MARKET STALL
KEEPER HAWKS
HIS CHEESES
AND MEATS
ROME

SAUTÉED VEAL AND HAM, ROMAN STYLE
SALTIMBOCCA ALLA ROMANA

A classic Italian dish suited to the simplest or the most elegant menu.

2 lbs. thinly sliced veal cutlets (8 slices)   8 tissue-thin slices prosciutto
salt, white pepper, and sage to taste   1/4 cup butter
1/2 cup finely minced parsley   1/3 cup Marsala wine

Have the butcher pound the meat to 1/16" thick. Season the veal with salt, pepper, sage, and parsley on both sides. Place a slice of ham, trimmed to precise fit, on each cutlet. Roll and tie with string or fasten with toothpicks. Sauté the rolls, a few at a time, in hot butter on all sides until golden. Remove to a warm platter and keep in a warm place while you cook the remaining rolls. Add the wine to the pan and increase the heat. Deglaze the pan, cooking rapidly for several minutes. Spoon this liquid over the veal and serve immediately. Serves 8.

BRAISED VEAL WITH BEANS
SPESSATINO DI VITELLO DELLA CASA

1 finely chopped onion
3 finely minced garlic cloves
3 tbs. butter
2 lbs. veal cut into 1" cubes
2 tbs. Marsala wine
1 cup chicken stock
3 tsp. tomato paste
salt
freshly ground pepper to taste
1 can well-drained white beans
1/4 cup finely minced parsley

Sauté onion and garlic in butter over medium heat until tender, not brown. Add the veal, tossing until it loses its raw look but do not brown it. Whisk together the wine, stock and tomato paste, blending into a smooth mixture. Add to the meat and season to taste. Cover and bake in a preheated 350° oven for 1 1/2 hours or until the meat is tender, not falling apart. Uncover and baste the meat with the juices during the cooking time. Add the well-drained beans and cook, covered, for 30 minutes longer. Adjust the seasoning, if necessary. Garnish each serving with parsley. Serves 6.

TRIPE, ROMAN STYLE
TRIPPA ALLA ROMANA

This recipe gives tripe a flavor well worth the additional time required for preparation.

3 lbs. honeycomb tripe
1 whole onion
2 minced cloves of garlic
salted water
2 tbs. olive oil
1/4 lb. chopped blanched lean salt pork
1 finely chopped onion
2 minced cloves of garlic

2 tbs. minced parsley
salt
freshly ground pepper to taste
3 cups chicken stock
2 tbs. flour
2 tbs. butter at room temperature
1/2 cup Meat Sauce (p.58)
1 cup grated Pecorino cheese

Scrub the tripe thoroughly under cold running water. Soak overnight in water to cover. Drain and cut into 1 1/2" squares. Place the tripe in a large pot with the whole peeled onion and garlic. Add salted water to generously cover the

tripe. Cover and pot and bring to a boil. Lower the heat and simmer for 3 hours. Drain the tripe and set aside. Sauté the salt pork, onions, garlic, and parsley in the hot oil using a large heavy-bottomed pan over medium heat. When the mixture is golden, add the tripe, season it, and brown on both sides. Add the chicken stock and bring to a boil. Reduce the heat to the lowest setting, cover, and simmer for 4 to 5 hours. Using a slotted spoon, remove the tripe to a warm platter. Boil the stock over high heat until there are barely 2 cups remaining.

Meanwhile, knead the flour into the softened butter and form into small balls. Reduce the heat under the stock to low. As the stock is simmering, add 1 ball of flour and butter at a time to the hot stock, stirring continuously with a whisk. Simmer for 5 minutes, stirring constantly. Add the Meat Sauce and continue cooking for 10 minutes. Taste and adjust the seasoning if necessary. Add the tripe to the sauce and simmer for several minutes. Serve in a warmed bowl. The grated Pecorino cheese should accompany the tripe and each diner garnishes as desired. Serves 6 generously.

SAUTÉED LAMB WITH POTATOES
SAUTÉ D'AGNELLO CON PATATE

one 5 to 6 lb. lamb leg
1/4 cup butter
2 tbs. olive oil
1 1/2 lbs. potatoes prepared as Potato Balls (p.115)
freshly ground pepper to taste

salt
1 cup dry white wine
1/2 cup canned beef gravy
1/2 cup Tomato Sauce (p.67)
1/4 cup finely minced parsley

Have the butcher bone the lamb leg. Then, using a boning knife, remove the fell and as much fat and muscle as possible. Slice the lamb 1/2" thick. Cut into strips about 2" long. Heat the butter and oil in a large heavy skillet over high heat. Sauté the lamb, a few pieces at a time so they are not crowded into the pan, browning the strips on all sides. They should be pink on the inside. Place the lamb on a large warm platter and season with salt and pepper. Keep warm in a 200° oven. Continue to sauté the lamb strips until all the meat has been prepared. Arrange the hot, cooked potato balls around the lamb on the platter. Add the wine, gravy, and tomato sauce to the skillet and cook over high heat until there are barely 1 1/3 cups of sauce remaining. Spoon the sauce over the lamb, garnish the potatoes with parsley, and serve immediately. Makes 6 servings.

ROASTED POTATO BALLS
COCCOLI DI PATATE

2 lbs. new potatoes   1 tbs. oil
2 tbs. butter

Peel the potatoes, pat dry and cut into tiny balls. Heat the butter and oil in a large heavy skillet over medium-high heat. Add the potato balls in a single layer. Shake the skillet to rotate the potatoes, browning them on all sides. Continue cooking for 5 more minutes, shaking the skillet several times. Reduce the heat to medium, cover, and cook for 10 to 15 minutes. Shake the skillet every few minutes. The potatoes are done when a sharp knife can pierce them easily.

LAMB, TUSCANY STYLE
AGNELLO CON PISELLI ALLA TOSCANA

one 6 to 7 lb. lamb leg
3 peeled cloves of garlic
1 1/2 tsp. dried rosemary
coarse salt
6 tbs. olive oil
6 large, peeled, seeded, diced, ripe tomatoes
water
salt
freshly ground pepper to taste
3 10-oz. pkgs. frozen peas

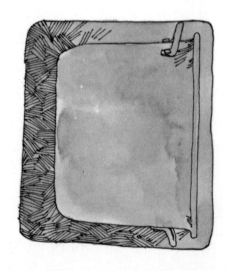

Have the butcher bone and roll the lamb leg. Use the tip of a sharp, thin knife to make small slits, evenly spaced, all around the leg. Slice the garlic cloves and coat them with rosemary. Insert a garlic slice in each slit. Rub the leg with a generous amount of salt. Heat the oil in a heavy pot which is just large enough to

hold the meat. When the oil is smoking, add the lamb and brown well on all sides. Distribute the tomatoes around the meat. Add enough water to cover 1/3 of the way up the side of the meat. Season the tomatoes with salt and pepper. Bring the water to a boil, cover the pot, and place in a preheated 300° oven. Simmer for about 2 1/2 hours, turning the lamb every 30 minutes for even cooking. Baste and add a little water if it looks dry. The meat is done when it is easily pierced by a cooking fork. About 15 to 20 minutes before the meat will be done, add the peas and about 1/4 cup water. Slice the lamb about 1/4" thick on a hot platter and spoon the sauce with the peas over and around the meat. Serves 6.

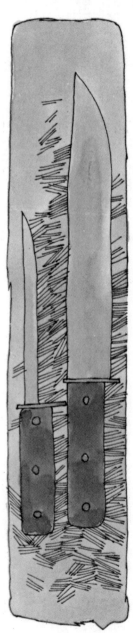

LAMB WITH SAUCE BOLOGNESE
SAUTÉ D'AGNELLO ALLA BOLOGNESE

Italians know that lamb served rare is a gourmet treat. It tastes completely different from the well-done version.

one 5 to 6 lb. lamb leg
1/4 cup butter
2 tbs. olive oil
salt
freshly ground pepper
1 1/4 cups dry red wine
3/4 cup Sauce Bolognese (p.70)
1/4 cup finely minced parsley

Have the butcher bone the lamb. Remove the fell and as much of the fat and muscles as possible, using a sharp boning knife. Cut the lamb into slices 1/2" thick. Cut the slices into 2" long strips. Heat the butter and oil over medium-high

heat in a large heavy skillet. When it sizzles, add just enough meat to easily brown in a single layer without crowding. Turn strips to brown on all sides. The strips should be pink in the center after browning. Using a slotted spoon, remove the meat to a warm platter. Season it lightly to taste with salt and pepper and keep warm in a 200° oven. Continue to quickly sauté the lamb until all the strips are done. Use more butter and oil if needed. Add the wine and Sauce Bolognese to the skillet and cook over high heat until you have barely 1 1/3 cups of sauce remaining. Spoon sauce over the meat, sprinkle with parsley, and serve immediately. Serves 6.

BONELESS CHICKEN BREAST WITH MUSHROOMS
FILETTO DI POLLO CON FUNGHI

1/2 lb. sliced fresh mushrooms
3 tbs. butter
6 boned chicken breasts
juice of 1 lemon

salt, freshly ground pepper to taste
5 tbs. butter
1/4 cup canned beef gravy
1 cup heavy cream

Use a medium-size skillet over medium heat to sauté the mushrooms in 3 tablespoons butter until tender. Remove from the heat and set aside. Sprinkle the chicken breasts with lemon juice, season lightly with salt and pepper, and rub gently into the chicken. Heat the 5 tablespoons butter in a large skillet. Quickly turn the chicken in the butter to completely coat the pieces. Cover the skillet and bake in a preheated 400°oven for 6 to 8 minutes. The chicken should feel slightly springy when you press it with a finger. Place the breasts on 6 warmed dinner plates. Add the beef gravy to the skillet and bring almost to a boil. Add the cream and cook at the same high heat until the sauce begins to thicken, then add the mushrooms. Season to taste. Spoon some sauce over each chicken breast. Serves 6.

HOUSES WALLING PORTOVENERE'S HARBOR FRONT FORMED STOUT DEFENSES AGAINST INVADERS DURING THE MIDDLE AGES.

MAMA GINA'S SPECIALTY
DELIZIE DI "MAMMA GINA"

Florentine food ranks with its art collections and this entree is sheer artistry.

6 chicken livers
3 tbs. butter
3 slices firm bread
milk
5 oz. ground veal
1/2 cup grated Parmesan cheese
grated rind of half a lemon
2 large beaten eggs

salt
freshly ground pepper to taste
6 large slices Prague ham cut 1/8" thick
6 tbs. butter
1 tbs. olive oil
2 1/2 cups Cream Sauce (p.62)
1/2 cup freshly grated Parmesan cheese
1 1/2 cups cooked, drained tiny peas

Trim chicken livers of any fat or membranes. Wash and thoroughly dry them on paper towels. Sauté in melted butter over medium heat until completely cooked, about 10 to 15 minutes. Set aside to cool, then chop. Soak bread in milk and squeeze dry. Put veal and bread through a grinder using the fine blade. Add

chicken livers, cheese, lemon rind, eggs, salt and pepper to veal. Mix thoroughly. divide the veal mixture into 6 parts, forming each into a log-like form. Place each log on a slice of ham. Roll up, first folding in both ends so the filling is completely enclosed, and secure the seam with a toothpick. Combine butter and oil in a heavy skillet over medium-high heat. When hot, brown the rolls. Reduce heat to low and and keep rolls warm. Meanwhile you have prepared Cream Sauce. Add Parmesan cheese and peas to the hot cream sauce. Serve rolls on warmed plates, spooning a generous 1/2 cup of sauce over each serving. Serves 6.

MIXED SEAFOOD FRY, SORRENTO STYLE
FRITTO MISTO SORRENTO

In Southern Italy, Fritto Misto usually means fried seafood—and to the diner, it means delicious feasting.

1/2 cup sifted flour
6 large eggs
1/2 tsp. salt
a few drops tabasco sauce
1 to 1 1/3 cups half and half
18 shelled deveined jumbo shrimp
1 1/2 lbs. shelled deveined medium shrimp
2 doz. shelled clams
2 doz. shelled oysters or mussels
1 lb. smelts
2 lbs. of several kinds of white-fleshed fish
18 lemon wedges

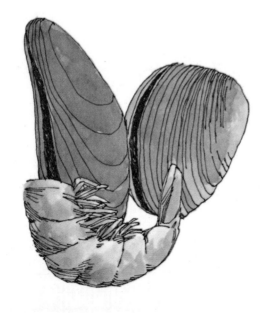

Place the first 5 ingredients in the blender. Using high speed, mix for 10 minutes. Pour the batter into a bowl, cover, and refrigerate for 2 hours. When you are ready to use the batter, beat with a rotary blender to prevent the flour from settling on the bottom of the bowl.

Have the fish clean and thoroughly dry. Heat vegetable oil in a deep fat dryer to 375°. Dip the fish and seafood in the batter just before you fry it, coating it completely and evenly. Fry a few pieces at a time, turning them to brown evenly. Remove from the fryer when the seafood is golden brown. Drain on paper towels and keep warm on a platter in a 250° oven. When all the seafood has been cooked, garnish with lemon wedges and serve. Makes 6 servings.

SHRIMP PILAF, PEOCETO STYLE
PILAF SCAMPI PEOCETO

Venetians exercise their culinary imagination with their favorite seafood—shrimp!

4 tbs. butter
2 cups raw Italian rice cooked al dente

Gently mix the butter into the cooked rice, and lightly pack into a buttered 2-quart bowl. Let stand about 1 minute. Invert onto a heated platter and serve with some of the sauce spooned over it and the remaining sauce in a warm serving bowl. Makes 6 generous servings.

Sauce

1 1/2 lbs. raw, shelled, deveined medium shrimp

flour

2 large peeled, seeded, diced, ripe tomatoes

3 tbs. well-drained capers

3 tbs. finely minced parsley

1/4 cup sweet butter

3 tbs. cognac

2 tbs. flour

2 cups light cream or half and half

Roll shrimp in flour. Shake off excess and place on a sheet of waxed paper. Continue until all the shrimp have been floured. Melt the butter in a skillet over medium heat and sauté the shrimp until lightly browned. Add the cognac, heat, and flame. When the flames have died down, remove the shrimp to a bowl and add the tomatoes, capers, and parsley to the skillet. Sauté for several minutes until the tomatoes have released some juice. Sprinkle the flour evenly over the skillet contents, stirring well with a whisk. Add the cream and cook until thickened. Return the shrimp to the sauce and simmer over the lowest heat for 5 minutes. Serve over rice. Serves 6.

PIAZZA SAN MARCO
VENICE

Breads

Fresh—and still hot—bread and rolls may be purchased direct from the bakeries and nowhere will you find packaged or sliced bread in Italy. Their breads are still free from the preservatives to be found in most bakery products sold in American markets.

Bread is present at every Italian meal. For the tiny breakfast, espresso is served with either rolls and sweet butter or cornetti. The bread is of high quality, firm with a crisp crust. It is made with flour having a high gluten content, giving the best texture. When you order espresso or capuccino for a mid-morning snack, cornetti—salty or sweet—are a standard in the pastry case.

These bread recipes are designed to free you from the necessity of constant checking to see if the dough has risen sufficiently. They are easy to prepare and extremely reliable for achieving delicious results.

ROLLS
PANINI

These are served at breakfast with sweet butter, jam, and espresso. They may also be served with lunch and dinner.

2 cups flour
2 pkgs. dry yeast
1 tbs. salt
2 tsp. sugar
2 tbs. butter at room temperature
2 1/4 cups hot water
4 cups flour
cold water

Combine the 2 cups flour, yeast, salt, and sugar in a large mixing bowl. Add the butter and hot water. Beat, using the medium speed of an electric mixer, for 2 minutes. Scrape the bowl several times during beating. Add 1 more cup of flour

and beat on the highest speed for 1 minute. The dough will be thick, smooth, and elastic. Add enough of the remaining flour to make the dough leave the sides of the bowl. Remove the dough to a floured pastry board and knead it for 10 minutes. This means punching the dough with your fist while making a turning motion. Give the dough a quarter turn, fold in half, punch, turn, and so on. Replenish the flour on the board as needed. Kneading eliminates air holes in the bread, giving it a firm, even texture.

Form the dough into a ball and cover with plastic wrap and a linen towel. Let rest for 20 minutes away from drafts. Uncover, punch down, and divide into 2 parts. Roll one piece of dough on the floured pastry board into an 8" x 18" rectangle. Cut the dough into 18 rectangles, each measuring about 2" x 4". Roll up with the short side toward you. Place seam side down on a greased cookie sheet about 2" apart to allow for spreading during baking. Cover with plastic wrap and refrigerate.

Place the second piece of dough on the board. Divide into 18 equal pieces.

Form each into a smooth ball. Place on another greased cookie sheet about 2" apart. Cover with plastic wrap. Refrigerate.

These rolls should be refrigerated for 3 to 6 hours. When you are ready to bake them, preheat the oven to 400°, remove the rolls from the refrigerator, and let them set at room temperature away from drafts for 10 minutes. Just before baking, cut a cross about 1/4" deep in the top of each ball of dough. Brush all the rolls with cold water. This produces a crisp crust. Bake for 15 to 25 minutes until browned. Tap one on the bottom—it should sound hollow. If not, continue to bake for 5 to 10 minutes. Immediately remove the rolls to a rack when done. Serve slightly warm with sweet butter and jams. Makes 36. These freeze and re-heat beautifully.

HARD ROLLS
PANINI DURI

The difference with these rolls is in the shape. They resemble a twisted Y. Use the dough in the recipe on page 130, following the recipe to the point where the rolls are formed. Divide the dough in half. Using a floured pastry board, roll the dough into a rectangle 8″ x 18″. Cut into 18 rectangles. Make a lengthwise cut about 2 1/2″ long. Twist each branch and the base, separate them—forming a Y shape—and pinch the end of each twisted coil to hold its shape.

Place the rolls on a greased cookie sheet and cover with plastic wrap. Repeat with the second piece of dough. Refrigerate for 3 to 6 hours. Preheat the oven to 400°. Remove the rolls from refrigerator and let stand at room temperature for 10 minutes. Just before baking, brush them with cold water. Bake for 20 to 25 minutes until browned and crisp. Immediately remove to a rack and cool. Makes 36.

SWEET CRESCENTS
DOLCE CORNETTI

My favorite breakfast is espresso and sweet cornetti. It beats toast!

2 cups flour
2 pkgs. dry yeast
1 1/2 tsp. salt
1/2 cup sugar
1/2 cup butter at room temperature
1 1/2 cups hot water
2 eggs at room temperature
4 cups flour
1/2 cup apricot jam
oil (not olive oil)

Glaze

1 large egg
1 tbs. water
1 tsp. sugar
1 tsp. oil

Combine the 2 cups of flour, yeast, salt, and sugar in a large mixing bowl. Add butter and water. Using an electric mixer, beat the dough at medium speed for 2

minutes, scraping the bowl several times. Add another cup of flour and the eggs. Beat on high speed for 1 minute until the dough is smooth and elastic. Beat in flour as needed until the dough leaves the side of the bowl. Turn the dough onto a floured pastry board and knead for 10 minutes. Form into a ball, cover with plastic wrap and a linen towel, and let the dough stand at room temperature for 20 minutes. Uncover and punch down. Divide in half and, on a floured board, roll 1 piece of dough into a rectangle 8" x 20". Cut into 10 squares about 4" on each side. Cut these in half diagonally and on each triangle place a tiny dab of jam. Roll from the wide part to the point, keeping the point underneath. Curve into a crescent and place on a greased cookie sheet about 2" apart. Repeat with the second piece of dough. Cover the cornetti with plastic wrap and refrigerate from 3 to 6 hours. Preheat the oven to 375°. Remove the cookie sheets from the refrigerator. Let stand for 10 minutes. Combine the glaze ingredients with a whisk and just before baking, brush each cornetti with the glaze. Bake for 20 to 25 minutes until browned and completely done. Cool on racks. Makes about 40.

THE COLOSSEUM
1,900 YEARS OLD
ROME

LAURIE'S FAVORITE CRESCENTS
CORNETTI (FAVORITO DI LAURIE'S)

Use the recipe for Sweet Cornetti (pp.134, 135) with these changes. Reduce the sugar to 2 tablespoons and eliminate the jam and glaze. When the cornetti are ready to be baked, brush them with 2 slightly beaten egg whites and roll in kosher (very coarse) salt. Complete Laurie's Cornetti as in the recipe for the sweet ones. Delicious with sweet butter.

A SIGNORINA SELECTS A BUNCH OF GRAPES

FRUIT BREAD
PANETTONE

This is a rich dough similar to brioche, laden with candied peel and raisins.

1/3 cup white raisins
1/3 cup dark raisins
1/4 cup dark rum
2 cups flour
2 pkgs. dry yeast
1/2 cup sugar
1 1/2 tsp. salt
1 1/2 tsp. cinnamon

grated rind of 2 lemons
1/2 cup butter at room temperature
1 1/3 cups hot water
4 large eggs at room temperature
5 cups flour
1/2 cup finely chopped candied orange peel
1/4 cup melted butter

Soak raisins in rum overnight. Drain, pat dry on paper towels, and set aside to use later. Combine the flour, yeast, sugar, salt, cinnamon, and lemon peel in a large mixing bowl. Add the butter and hot water. Using an electric mixer on medium speed, beat for 2 minutes, scraping the bowl several times. Add the eggs

and 1 1/2 cups flour, then beat at high speed for 1 minute. Add as much of the remaining flour as needed to get the dough to leave the sides of the bowl. Turn onto a floured pastry board and knead for 10 minutes. Form into a ball and cover with plastic wrap and a linen towel. Let the dough rest for 20 minutes away from drafts. Punch down, add the chopped peel and the raisins, and divide the dough into 2 equal pieces. Form each piece into a smooth ball and place each one on a separate greased cookie sheet. Cut 2 strips of brown paper 5'' wide and 25'' long. Butter the paper on one side and loosely wrap each strip around each ball of dough, buttered side in. Fasten the paper collar with a pin or paper clip. Each collar should be about 6'' to 8'' in diameter. Cover the panettone with plastic wrap and refrigerate. Preheat the oven to 425°. Remove dough from refrigerator and let stand for 10 minutes. Just before baking cut a cross about 1/4'' deep on top of each loaf. Generously brush loaves with melted butter, bake for 8 minutes, then reduce heat to 350° and bake an additional 35 to 45 minutes. When done, remove the paper collar and cool on a rack. Makes 2 panettone. Freezes beautifully.

SOME MUSSELS FOR
A MEAL ~ SORRENTO

Pizza

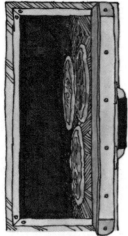

In general, food is served in Italy with style. Formica and paper plates seem not to have arrived yet, thank goodness. Coffee is always served in a real cup—not a paper one! The city of Venice, in particular, has many cafes and restaurants as it is a city catering to many visitors. Everywhere you go are cafes to tease your appetite, with people sitting at outside tables eating pizza, drinking coffee, or having soft drinks. Some have magnificent collections of art—oils, lithographs, and woodcuts, including mobiles and sculpture—which it is said that the artists gave to the owners in place of paying their checks. These cafes may also display their wines for all to see as well as sausages, salads, and a large variety of snack foods.

Americans are likely to have several quick meals—lunches, snacks, TV nibbles, or other between-meal food—rather than the large lengthy meals the Italians enjoy; therefore, pizza has been adopted throughout this country as the ideal

quick lunch food, being tasty, satisfying, and easily concocted (if you can keep the dough handy in the refrigerator).

Pizza is also considered a snack food in Italy. You may order it for a quick lunch in a cafe or as a light late evening meal. Many restaurants in Rome, for example, begin serving pizza after midnight. It is always served in individual pizzas about 6" in diameter. It is not sectioned for your convenience nor is it to be eaten out-of-hand, but is served whole and is eaten using a knife and fork.

Pizza toppings are more varied than those served in American pizzerias and the ingredients are not cut into tiny pieces, but are larger and therefore more noticeable, more identifiable, and tastier.

The recipes in this section will enhance your meals, your "snack cuisine," or your after-theater party, and can bring a touch of Italy to the simplest occasion.

PIZZA, VENETIAN STYLE
PIZZA VENEZIANA

Try this recipe the next time you have a yen for pizza. WOW!

Dough

1 pkg. dry yeast
3/4 cup warm water
1 tsp. salt
3 1/2 cups flour

Topping

olive oil
1 lb. peeled, seeded, ripe tomatoes
3 cooked mild Italian sausages
1 tbs. well-drained capers
2 tsp. dried basil
1 1/2 doz. scrubbed, steamed, shelled mussels
1/2 lb. shredded mozzarella cheese

Soften the yeast in the water. Combine the flour and salt in a large bowl, make a well in the center, and pour the yeast into it. Use your hand to knead the ingredients into a smooth dough, adding a little water if needed to get a smooth, fairly soft dough. Shape the dough into a ball and place it in a greased bowl. Cover and store in a warm, draft-free place until the dough has risen to double its original size. Turn the dough onto a floured pastry board, punch it down, and knead it several times. Divide the dough into 6 equal pieces. Roll or pat each piece of dough into a 6" circle (diameter) about 1/8" thick. Shape a rim on each circle. The rim should be upturned and slightly thicker than the rest of the circle. Place the circles on 2 large oiled cookie sheets and brush the surface of each circle with oil. Cut the tomatoes into thin strips and evenly divide them among the 6 pizzas. Remove the casing from the sausage, crumble it, and divide equally among the pizza. Sprinkle the capers, basil, and 3 mussels on each pizza. Finally, evenly divide the cheese on top of each pizza. Bake in a preheated 450° oven for 10 to 15 minutes and serve immediately on 6 hot plates. Each pizza is an individual serving.

JULIA'S PIZZA
PIZZA GIULIA

The unusual egg garnish adds a special touch to this pizza.

Pizza dough (p.143)
olive oil
3/4 cup sliced green onions
1/2 cup chopped green pepper
1 1/8 cups cooked tiny shrimp

1 lb. peeled, seeded, chopped, ripe tomatoes
2/3 cup finely minced salami
2 tsp. dried oregano
1 1/2 cups shredded mozzarella cheese
6 peeled, quartered, hard-cooked eggs

Prepare the dough and shape as directed, placing the 6 circles on 2 oiled cookie sheets. Sauté the green onions and peppers in 2 tablespoons oil. Brush each circle with oil. Evenly divide the tomatoes among the pizzas, then spoon on the onions, green peppers, shrimp, and salami. Season with oregano and sprinkle with the cheese. Bake in a preheated 450° oven for 10 to 15 minutes. Arrange a quartered egg in the center of each pizza. Serve immediately on 6 hot plates.

STUFFED PIZZA
CALZONE IMBOTTITO

This resembles a stuffed pizza or pasty.

1 cup flour
1 pkg. dry yeast
2 tsp. sugar
2 tsp. salt
2 tbs. margarine at room temperature
1 1/8 cups hot water

2 1/2 cups flour
melted bacon fat
3 oz. diced salami
6 slices mozzarella cheese
1 large egg
1 tsp. water

Combine the flour, yeast, sugar, and salt in a large mixing bowl. Add the margarine and hot water to the dry ingredients. Beat, using the mixer on medium speed for 2 minutes, scraping the bowl several times. Add 1/2 cup flour and beat for 1 minute at high speed. Add as much of the remaining flour as the dough needs to make it leave the sides of the bowl. Knead the dough on a floured board for 8 to 10 minutes, then form into a ball and cover with plastic wrap and a linen

towel. Let the dough rest for 20 minutes. Punch down and divide into 6 parts. Roll out each part to about 1/8" thick and 6" to 8" in diameter. Brush with melted bacon fat. Put a slice of mozzarella and some diced salami in the center of each circle of dough. Beat the egg and water together, brush the edges of each circle with the egg mixture, and fold each in half. Seal by crimping with a fork to be certain the filling will not escape. Place the Calzone on 2 greased cookie sheets, cover with plastic wrap, and refrigerate for 3 to 6 hours. Preheat the oven to 400°. Let the Calzone set at room temperature for 10 minutes before baking. Just before placing in the oven, brush each turnover with melted fat. Bake in a 400° oven for 25 to 30 minutes. Serve immediately. Makes 6 Calzone.

147

CAMOGLI
REKNOWNED DURING
THE 19TH CENTURY AS -
THE PORT OF 1,000 SAILS

Desserts

Desserts—rich, sweet, creamy, lucious and undeniably fattening—were born in Italy. Probably the word "French" comes automatically to mind when pastries are mentioned but the French chefs only refined the art. Actually, the art of pastry and desserts was brought to France when Catherine de Medici came to Paris to claim (or be claimed by) her bridegroom, the future Henry II, and just incidentally brought her personal pastry chef along. The ancestry of such desserts as custards, fruit ices, pastry creams, puddings, and rich purees of all kinds belong irrefutably to the Italians—they are indeed the founders of "la dolce vita."

The same concern for color and beauty in the rest of the menu extends to desserts and the ice cream concoctions are no exception. Ice cream is very popular in Italy and most good restaurants make their own.

The desserts in this section will appeal to your eye and your appetite. They are delicious as the finale to a meal or as elegant treats with coffee.

MOCK GENOISE
PAN DI SPAGNA IMITATO

Rich sponge-like cake is the basis of many Italian desserts. This recipe is an easier, almost fool-proof version.

2/3 cup sifted flour
1 tsp. baking powder
1/4 tsp. salt
4 large eggs
3/4 cup sugar
1 1/2 tsp. vanilla

Sift together the flour, baking powder, and salt. Line the bottom of a greased 15" x 10" x 1" jelly roll pan with waxed paper. Grease the paper. Separate the egg yolks and whites, putting the whites into a large clean mixing bowl. Remember that the bowl, beaters, and whisk must be thoroughly clean to get the best volume from the whites. Use an electric mixer at high speed to beat the egg

whites, gradually adding **1/2 cup sugar**, beating well after each addition. After sugar has been added, stiff peaks should form when the beaters are raised. Next beat the egg yolks at high speed, gradually adding the remaining 1/4 cup sugar and the vanilla. The mixture will become very thick. Use a whisk to fold the egg yolk mixture and the flour into the beaten egg whites, whisking gently just until no more flour can be seen. Pour the batter into the prepared pan, gently leveling it. Bake in a preheated 375° oven for 10 to 12 minutes. Use a sharp knife to cut the sides of the cake from the pan and turn onto a damp linen dish towel. Use the cake as soon as it is cool as it becomes stale very quickly.

RUM CUSTARD CAKE
ZABAIONE DI RUM DEL GRILLO

The term "Zabaglione" as used in this recipe refers to the rum cream.

Double recipe Mock Genoise (p.150)
Rich Custard (p.153)
1/4 cup dark rum

1 cup heavy cream, whipped
8 oz. sweet chocolate, chilled

Halve both cakes crosswise. Set one piece aside for other use. Add the rum to the custard, whisking until smooth. Place one square of cake in a shallow dish and spread with 1/2 of the rum custard. Carefully place another layer of cake on the custard and spread with the remaining custard. Set the last piece of cake on top. Swirl the whipped cream on this. Use a vegetable peeler to create chocolate curls. Cover your work surface with waxed paper, then peel the chocolate along the longest smooth surface to create the chocolate curls. Heap these on top of the whipped cream. Try not to handle the curls too much—they crumble easily. Serves 8 to 10.

QUICK CUSTARD
CREMA RAPIDO

4 1/2 oz. pkg. vanilla pudding mix
1 cup heavy cream
1 cup half and half or light cream

Combine all ingredients using a whisk. Cook in a heavy-bottomed saucepan over medium heat until it just comes to a boil. Use the whisk constantly. Cover the surface of the custard with waxed paper to prevent formation of a skin. Cool. Refrigerate if you are not serving it immediately after cooling period.

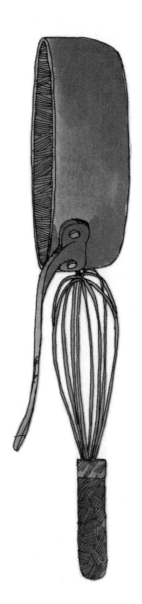

ICE CREAM DESSERT, FLORENTINE STYLE
ZUCOTTO ALLA FIORENTINA

We savored this rich dessert at the 13 Gobbi restaurant in Florence.

1 recipe Mock Genoise (p.150)
Kirsch or Maraschino liqueur
1 pt. softened rich vanilla ice cream
1/3 cup chopped candied pineapple
1 pt. softened rich chocolate ice cream
2/3 cup coarsely chopped bittersweet chocolate

Use a 1-quart hard plastic bowl about 4 1/2" deep. I like the Tupperware 1-quart mixing bowl. Cut a circle of spongecake 4" in diameter and place it in the bottom of the bowl. Cut a strip of spongecake 5" by 15" and use this to line the sides of the bowl. Fill in any gaps with additional cake. Generously sprinkle the cake in the bowl with Kirsch or Maraschino. Quickly mix the chopped chocolate into the ice cream. Carefully spoon the chocolate ice cream evenly into the cake-

lined bowl, making sure there are no air pockets. Level it. Cover the bowl and place it in the freezer while you prepare the vanilla ice cream.

Mix the candied fruit into the softened vanilla ice cream and spoon it evenly over the chocolate ice cream in the bowl. Cut a circle of spongecake exactly 5 1/2" in diameter to fit the top of the bowl. Place the cake circle on the ice cream and sprinkle it generously with the liqueur. The cake should come right to the top of the bowl. Cover the bowl with either foil or the regular cover and place in a 0° freezer until completely firm. To be completely secure, prepare this either early in the day or the night before. When ready to serve the Zucotto, immerse a linen dish towel in hot water and wring out all the excess. Uncover the bowl, place it upside down on a serving dish and wrap the hot towel around it. It should unmold easily. If not, cover it and dunk the bowl quickly in and out of a pot of hot water being careful not to get any water into the Zucotto. Serves 6.

ORANGE DUCHESS
ARANCIA DUCHESSE

This unusual dessert is a specialty of Ristorante Peoceto Risorto in Venice.

1/4 cup canned Queen Anne cherries, well-drained
1 tbs. Kirsch
1 slice canned pineapple, well-drained
1 fresh navel orange
1/3 cup fresh strawberries, halved
1 cooked peach half
1 large fresh strawberry (garnish)
1 tbs. Kirsch

Marinate the cherries in the Kirsch overnight. Drain before using. Place the pineapple slice in a shallow coupe dish and arrange the halved strawberries around the pineapple. Peel a navel orange, very carefully removing all traces of the white inner rind. Cut into sections between the membranes, then, gently holding the

orange together, center it on the pineapple slice. Cap it with the peach half, cut side down. Anchor it to the orange with 2 wooden toothpicks near the center and place a large fresh strawberry on top of the toothpicks, hiding them from view. Place the cherries around the base of the orange. Pour the tablespoon of Kirsch over the dessert. Serves 1.

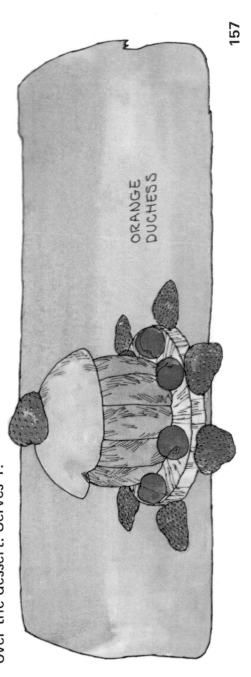

ORANGE DUCHESS

157

ICE CREAM SUNDAE, GOBBI STYLE
COUPE 13 GOBBI

I enjoyed a slightly different version of this recipe in the 13 Gobbi restaurant in Florence. Since homemade ice cream is not usually available here, I have taken a few liberties with the recipe.

1 slice canned pineapple packed in its natural juices
1 scoop pineapple ice cream
generous serving of whipped cream
1/4 cup bittersweet chocolate, coarsely chopped
2 tbs. chopped walnuts
1 tbs. Kahlua

Center the ice cream on the pineapple slice in a coupe dish and top with a generous serving of whipped cream. Cover with the chocolate and the walnuts. Pour the Kahlua over the top. Serves 1.

CHOCOLATE TRUFFLES
TARTUFI CIOCCOLATO

We sat at the Tre Scalini cafe in the Piazza Navona in Rome eating this luscious calorific sweet. Ummm, good!

6 large scoops of the richest chocolate ice cream available
6 maraschino cherries, well-drained
2 cups bittersweet chocolate, coarsely chopped
3/4 cup heavy cream, whipped

Imbed a cherry in the center of each ice cream ball. Thickly coat each scoop of ice cream with the chopped chocolate. Place each ice cream ball on a fluted paper cup. Freeze them until solid. Just before serving, pipe a rosette of whipped cream on each one. Serves 6.

WITH HIS PANTS
ROLLED UP, THE OLD
WINE MAKER TREADS
THE GRAPES JUST AS
HIS ANCESTORS DID.

Wines & Aperitifs

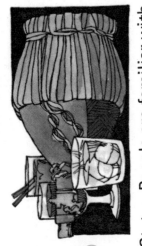

Italian wines are not well known in the United States. People are familiar with Chianti but many are bemused by fancy bottles. They are not generally knowledgeable about reliable labels and certainly not aware of the tremendous array of wines produced by Italy.

Italians are justly famous for their red wines. Like French red wines, it is recommended they be served at room temperature, which really means "cellar" temperature, or about 60° - 65°. The bouquet of red wines is enhanced if the cork is removed at least two hours before serving. Some older red wines may have considerable sediment and, if so, leave the bottle upright for at least 24 hours and open by carefully easing out the cork, leaving the sediment relatively undisturbed.

For an introduction to the finest in Italian wines, I recommend that you shop at a store with a knowledgeable proprietor. Ask for his recommendations. Some Italian wines usually available in the U.S. are described on the following pages.

RED WINES
VINO ROSSO

BARBARESCO—Ruby red color, aroma like violets, smooth, tangy, medium dry. Best at 3 years of age. Serve at room temperature (65°).

BARBERA—Deep ruby red. Bouquet of both violets and delicate Italian cherries. Full bodied, hearty. Drinkable until 3 years old. Serve at room temperature with well-seasoned, robust food.

BARDOLINO—Clear ruby color, delicate bouquet, semi-dry. Best when young. Serve at room temperature. Good with veal, lean beef, and chicken.

BAROLO—Dry, rich, and hearty; luscious ruby color. Should be at least 4 years old. Serve at room temperature. Best with roast beef and lamb.

CHIANTI—Dry, tangy, hearty, with a delightful bouquet. Should be at least 3 years old. Serve at room temperature. Best with roast beef and lamb.

GRIGNOLINO—Lovely bouquet, light, dry. Should be 2 years old. Serve at room temperature. Best served with the main course.

VALPOLICELLA—Dry, light and smooth. Usually best when young. Serve at room temperature. Another good all-around table wine.

WHITE WINES
VINO BIANCO

SOAVE—A straw-colored, dry wine. It is delicate, should be well-chilled. Serve with antipasto and fish courses. Similar to Chablis.

ORVIETO—Pale, delicate, with a lovely bouquet. Full-bodied and dry. Serve well-chilled with fish and delicate pasta dishes.

CORVO—Golden color, a magnificent bouquet, velvety taste. Serve well-chilled with fish and antipasto.

CASTELLI ROMANI—Should be at least 6 years old. Make sure it is the dry version. Very smooth. Serve cold with fish.

LACRIMI CHRISTI—Amber-colored, very delicate bouquet, a medium-dry wine. Serve chilled. Best with fish. Be careful to ask your wine dealer to recommend a reliable shipper. This is not a "protected" name and many wines bearing this name are overpriced and of indifferent quality.

VERDICCHIO—Clear, pale amber, dry. Very delicate bouquet. Serve chilled. Delightful with antipasto and fish. It should be drunk while it is 1 to 3 years old.

SWEET WINES
DOLCE VINO

EST EST EST—Straw-colored, lovely perfumed bouquet. Best when 4 years old. The sweet variety has the flavor of the Muscat grape. Serve chilled.

MALVASIA DI LIPARI—Golden color, very subtle flavor. Should be 4 to 6 years old. Serve chilled with the bottle resting in ice.

MARSALA—Brown, sweet, "over the rocks" or chilled with a lemon twist.

MOSCATO DI PANTELLERIA—Golden-amber color, sweet and smooth, rich bouquet. Should be 5 to 6 years old. Serve very cold.

MOSCATE (ASTI) SPUMANTE—Sweet, delicate, bubbly. Best when 4 years old. Serve very cold.

VIA VENETO

2 oz. dry sherry
1 oz. Italian vermouth
a dash of orange bitters

Stir the ingredients with crushed ice and strain into a cocktail glass. Makes 1 drink.

ROMA

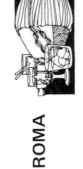

4 oz. Italian vermouth
1 oz. Fernet Branca (bitters)

Stir with crushed ice. Strain into a chilled wine glass. Makes 1 drink.

CAMPARI

Campari is a very popular "bitter" drink in Italy. Since it is not to everyone's liking, order a drink made with it in a bar to see if it suits your taste. It is found in the following drinks:

NEGRONI

1 oz. EACH of gin, sweet vermouth, soda and Campari
lemon or lime twist

Put a generous amount of ice in an 8-ounce glass. Add the gin, vermouth, and Campari with enough soda to fill the glass. Garnish with the lemon or lime twist. Makes 1 drink.

AMERICANO

3 oz. sweet vermouth
1 oz. Campari
soda
lemon twist

Put ice in an 8-ounce glass. Add the vermouth and Campari. Top off the glass with soda and garnish with the lemon twist. Makes 1 drink.

ITALIAN TYROL
ROADSIDE SHOP

Fruit & Cheeses

One of the most popular desserts in Italy is fruit and cheese. Fresh fruit of the season is attractively arranged in a bowl. You are provided with a plate about the size of a salad plate, a special fork and a sharp fruit knife. Fruit is never eaten out of hand. You must impale the fruit with the fork, quarter it, and proceed to peel it. Then you cut it into manageable pieces and it is ready to eat.

Cheeses are always served at room temperature. In many restaurants you are served sections of several kinds of cheese. Try to shop for Italian cheeses in an Italian neighborhood, as they will stock more varieties of Italian cheese and it will be fresher.

PARMESAN—This can be eaten with fruit provided you purchase ITALIAN Parmesan under the name PARMIGIANO-REGGIANO. This is stenciled on the rind. What passes as Parmesan domestically has no relation to the authentic Italian cheese.

GORGONZOLA—This is a veined cheese like Roquefort but with a much different flavor. The veining is light green and the cheese is rich and creamy. This applies only to the Italian Gorgonzola, not the domestic variety.

PROVOLONE—The name applies to the shape of the cheese—oval. When it is fresh it is mild, creamy, delightful. As it ages it resembles sheep's milk cheese. It becomes salty with a tangy taste.

TALEGGIO—This cheese should be bland and creamy. Smell it before buying and if it has the tartness of a Brie or Camembert, forget it.

FONTINA D'AOSTA—A cheese which resembles the best of Emmenthal (Swiss) cheese. The waxed rind should be a light, warm-brown color. Since the name Fontina is not restricted, take care not to buy others simply because they

carry the same or a similar name as it will not bear any resemblance to the genuine article.

BEL PAESE—A soft creamy cheese popular all over the United States. It has a distinctive wrapping showing a map. If it is the Italian cheese, the map is of Italy. If the cheese is domestic, the map is of the Americas. The imported version of the cheese is the better of the two, but if that is not available, you will find the American version quite delicious.

MOZZARELLA—In Southern Italy this cheese is made from buffalo's milk. The mozzarella available here is made from cow's milk. It is mild, tender and delicious. Incidentally, the name in Italy also applies to athletic teams who don't perform well or individual young men who don't live up to masculine standards.

THE BASILICA OF ST. PETER
VATICAN CITY - ROME

Coffee

Coffee was first brought to Italy in 1615 by Pietro della Valle. Many travelers in the Middle East learned to love coffee and imported it for their personal use. It was very rare, soon in great demand and, therefore, very expensive.

Coffee must be roasted before the aroma is released. The green coffee bean has no odor and keeps for a long time. For this reason, many coffee devotees perform the roasting operation themselves, thereby preserving the full flavor and aroma of the beans. Ideally, the coffee bean should be ground immediately before the coffee is brewed, since it quickly loses aroma after being ground.

Cafe au lait—or coffee with milk or cream—has reduced qualities of stimulation and actually becomes a food. Coffee is also used for flavoring a great number of dishes, but is probably most popular for flavoring desserts.

To an Italian, coffee IS espresso. Espresso is a very strong brew from a special bean, prepared with a machine (or machinetta) which forces steam through the

ground coffee. It is served in demitasse cups with sugar but no cream. It is very strong, just right to keep you "nervous." Espresso is never served with meals except at breakfast—not even with dessert. Italians prefer their coffee at the very end of the meal. Wine and mineral water accompany the meal.

Since an electric espresso machine is quite costly, there are other less expensive espresso machines available. They resemble coffee pots but are in three pieces. The water is in the bottom part, the coffee in the middle and the serving "pot" on top. When the water comes to a boil, the water is placed over the coffee and the "pot" is on the bottom. After the water drips through the coffee, the espresso is ready to serve in the "pot." Demitasse cups are only half-filled because this brew is so strong.

Cafe Cappuccino is made by combining steaming espresso with an equal quantity of steaming milk. Pour into tall cups and top with cinnamon, nutmeg, allspice—or even whipped cream, which children love as a hot drink.

INDEX